The MIRACLE of LOVE

written and
compiled by

DOUGLAS AND JEWEL BEARDALL

LDS BOOK PUBLICATIONS
-Provo, Utah-

The MIRACLE *of* LOVE

Other book
Publications by
Douglas and Jewel Beardall-

The Missionary Kit
The Qualities of Love
Death and the LDS Family
Mormon Money Matters
About the Three Nephites
Passage to Light
Cookbook for All Seasons

Tenth Printing - March 1993

Copyright © 1980 by Douglas Beardall
Published by LDS Book Publications
P.O. Box 1515, Provo, Utah 84603
(801) 226-3539
ISBN: 1-882371-01-1

Printed in The United States of America

This book is dedicated to our precious children

Jeff, Holly, Jennifer and Scott,

who are truly our

"Miracles of Love".

Thou shalt love the Lord
thy God with all thy
heart, and with all thy
soul, and with all thy mind.
(Matthew 22:37.)

Preface

N o principle of the gospel is emphasized more and understood less than the principle of love. Love is the first and greatest commandment. A complete understanding of love is essential to our salvation through Christ.

We have carefully selected and compiled works by some of our most loved and respected gospel authorities; leaders whom we feel have developed an understanding of the "Miracle of Love." Of course, the supreme teacher is Christ who demonstrates the total essence of love to everyone.

It is our hope that you may find peace, satisfaction, and a deeper understanding of love, to develop a personal Christlike "Miracle of Love," to enrich the lives of your family and friends.

Douglas and Jewel Beardall

CONTENTS

For God so loved the
world, that he gave
his only begotten Son.

(John 3:16)

Chapter One

Three Kinds of Love

C. Douglas Beardall

T here is hardly a person in the world who does not want to be loved. The security and satisfaction of being loved by someone is basic to a happy life.

Yes, we know very little about love or how to seek it. Rarely are we told in understandable terms what love is. Not many have attended a class on love or read a helpful book on it. This most important, indispensable thing in life has been strangely neglected in our education.

There are at least three kinds of love, although some persons may like to distinguish several more. One's happiness may depend on which of these types of love one is seeking.

The first is called the "if" kind of love. It is the love which will be given to us "if" we meet certain requirements. "If you are good, father will love you," "If you give me gifts, I will love you." "If you promise to marry me, I will give you my love." "If you become successful and important, I will love you." "If you come up to expectations as a husband, I will be your faithful wife." This is the most common kind of love, and some may not know any other kind. It is love with strings attached, the conditional love, the love offered in exchange for something the lover wants. It is motivational and selfish. Its purpose is to gain something in exchange for love.

The cheapest form of this kind of love is what we often meet in cheap movies, magazines, and novels. "If you satisfy my desire, I will love you." Many people, especially young people, don't realize that the love they expect to win from someone by satisfying his or her sexual demand is cheap, a form which cannot satisfy them and is not worth the price. Ammon, one of the sons of David, was attracted to his good-looking half sister, Tamare. He pretended to be sick and contrived to have her attend to him in his room. One day he took hold of her and said, "Come lie with me, my sister." But, she answered him, "No, my brother, do not force me; for such a thing is wanton folly." Nevertheless, he would not listen to her and laid with her. Then Ammon hated her exceedingly, so that the hatred with which he hated her was greater than the form of love with which he had loved her (Samuel 13:1-15). This form of love is so selfish that it quickly turns into hate in both partners.

Many marriages fail because they are founded on this "if" kind of love. The young bride or the groom is often in love not with the real, actual personality of the partner, but the imaginary, glorified personality of the partner. When disillusionment sets in and the expectations are not met, the former love turns to hate. Tragically, it may not have been their fault. They may not have known that there was any love other than the "if" kind of love.

Sometimes even parental love, usually considered the purest of human love, is no more than this "if" kind of love. A few years ago the suicide of a young lad made the front pages in the daily newspaper. Wanting to please his father by passing the entrance examinations to the university, against keen competition, he had studied very hard since his junior high school days, attending extra classes after school. But, he failed. Unable to face his father and wanting to drown his disappointment, he went to relax for a weekend at a nearby resort. When he returned home, he was confronted by his angry father. "Aren't you ashamed of yourself? Not only failing the examination but also going off on vacation!" the father reproached him. "But Dad, I thought you once said when you feel low you enjoy a vacation rest." The father had no reply to that and in his anger beat the boy severely. That night the boy disconnected the rubber gas tube which ran from the gas outlet on the wall to the gas heater, put the tube in his mouth to take in a lungful of gas, and killed himself. The newspaper simply said the suicide was due to a nervous breakdown. I think the breakdown was caused by the sudden realization that his father's love was conditional upon the boy's meeting his high expectations.

We are all looking for something more than this "if" kind of love. To learn that there is a truer love and to learn where it can be found may someday mean the difference between living out your life, and simply giving up as this boy did.

The second kind of love is called the "because" kind of love. In this love the person is loved because of something he is, something he does, something he has. There is a quality or condition in a person which makes someone love him. "I love you because you are so lovely." "I love you because you are good to me." "I love you because you are different than others, so popular, wealthy, and so famous." "I love you because you give me security." "I love you because you take me to such romantic places." We may laugh at some of these remarks, but we ourselves often love people because of some lovable quality we see in them.

To be loved in this way, however, soon becomes no better than trying to win the "if" kind of love. Since it feels so good to have someone love us because of what we are, we strive endlessly to add to our circle of admirers. Now if someone else should come along who has more of the lovable quality than we do, we would be afraid that those who love us would love this newcomer more. Thus, competition and endless effort to win love enters into our lives. The baby of the family resents the coming of another baby. The popular girl resents the new pretty girl in town. The young man resents another fellow with a flashier car. The wife resents the attractive, efficient secretary. Where is there security in this kind of love?

"Perfect love casteth out fear" (I John 4:18). Then this cannot be the true kind of love.

Besides the fear of competition, there are at least two other reasons why this "because" kind of love brings insecurity with it. First, it makes us afraid that we may not really be the lovable person our lover thinks we are. All men have two sides to their personality, to a greater or lesser extent. There is the side we show to people, and the other side only we ourselves know. We are constantly on guard to hide this second side for fear that those who love us may be disappointed and reject us.

Another reason for insecurity in this kind of love is the fear that some time in the future we may change and no longer be as lovable as we are.

Too much of love is of this kind, leaving us unsure of its permanence.

The third kind of love is called the "inspite of" love. It is different from the "if" kind of love in that it has no strings attached and expects nothing in return. It is different from the "because" kind of love in that it is not brought forth by some attractive quality in the person who is being loved. In this third kind of love, the person is loved "in spite of" not because of, what he is. One may be the most ugly, most wretched person in the world and would still be loved when he meets this "inspite of" kind of love. He does not have to deserve it. He does not have to earn it by being attractive or wealthy. He is simply loved as he is, in spite of the faults or ignorance or bad habits he may have. He may be loved as though he were of infinite worth. This is the kind of love for which our hearts are desperately hungry.

This kind of love is the most important. Suppose at this very moment you suddenly had a bitter quarrel with the person you cherished most and realized that he or she loved you only for what he could get out of you; wouldn't your life cloud up from the inside until you felt you could not go on another day? Even if you are somehow going along from day to day thinking yourself reasonably happy, could you live the rest of your life if there was no hope whatsoever that someday someone will love you with a true, deep, satisfying love?

You are getting along today either because you are receiving this "inspite of" kind of love from someone or

hoping to find it. But we cannot receive enough of this
kind of love to satisfy us fully. No one has a surplus to
give. We expect someone to give us this love, but that
person himself is also seeking it. In this world, we only
get enough of it to whet our appetites and to show us
how much we need it. The greatest scarcity in the world
exists in the realm of this "inspite of" kind of love.

It is the wonderful message of the scriptures that in
Christ this kind of love became available to man in satisfying fulness. God did not leave man empty in his long-
ing and hoping. He sent his Son into the world to bring
to each person more love. Through the coming of Christ,
for the first time in history, many were able to see and
feel this absolutely pure love with his own heart.

The love that Christ brings to us from God is not the
"if" kind of love. He loves all His children equally, without partiality. He does not say, I will love you if you are a
good and moral person, if you go to church, if you give
contributions, if you read the scriptures, or if you pray.
There are no "ifs" of any kind. He loves us as we are.
This love is our motivation to become more like Him. If
day by day we become more degenerate and rebellious,
he would still love us with the more complete love. He
does not love us for what He can get out of us. There is no
requirement we must meet, no condition to fulfill. Jesus
came into the world and lived out his mortal life in
goodness and love toward all men, especially giving
himself to the poor and despised from whom He could
expect nothing in return. He paid a high price for serving
those who had nothing to return to him. He was
criticized over and over again for mixing with the sick,
the poor, the uneducated, and the outcasts. Then in
obedience to God, He died on the cross for the sins of

mankind. Even while He was dying on the cross, He said of those who were putting him to death: "Father, forgive them for they know not what they do" (Luke 23:24). Just as Paul the Apostle said, "This is my commandment, That ye love one another, as I have loved you. Greater love hath no man than this, that a man lay down his life for his friends" (John 15:12-13). This is the genuine "in spite of" kind of love in all its fulness and purity.

Even today the only source of this "in spite of" love is Jesus Christ. Christ is the spring from which this stream of pure love constantly flows. This kind of love cannot be manufactured.

Trusting our welfare to God and thinking more about the welfare of others, we can establish our families, friendships and society on the basis of the "in spite of" type of love.

The proof that we have really received this pure love from God is our ability to love others no matter what. "We love because he first loved us" (I John 4:19). We can forgive those whom we could never forgive. God has filled us to overflowing with his own love. Having this relationship with God and offering loving service to men is the full and satisfying life we long for.

"Wherefore, my beloved brethren, pray unto the Father with all the energy of heart, that ye may be filled with this love, which he hath bestowed upon all who are true followers of his Son, Jesus Christ; that ye may become the sons of God; that when he shall appear we shall be like him, for we shall see him as he is; that we may have this hope, that we may be purified even as he is pure.   Amen" (Moroni 7:38).

IF I HAD KNOWN

If I had known what trouble you were bearing;
What griefs were in the silence of your face;
I would have been more gentle, and more caring,
And tried to give you gladness for a space.
I would have brought more warmth into the place,
   If I had known.

If I had known what thoughts despairing drew you;
(Why do we never try to understand?)
I would have lent a little friendship to you,
And slipped my hand within your hand,
And made your stay more pleasant in the land,
   If I had known.

MARY CAROLYN DAVIES

Chapter Two

Love One Another

N. Eldon Tanner

I contemplate conditions in the world that are causing so much unrest and unhappiness and then ask myself: What is our greatest need in order to meet these conditions and bring about a change so that we might enjoy peace and happiness?

My answer seemed to center on these two messages, taken from the teachings of the Lord Jesus Christ: "Seek ye first the kingdom of God, and his righteousness; and all these things shall be added unto you," and "Love one another."

In these two statements can be found the key to the solution of all those problems which are causing such misery and trouble for individuals, communities, nations, and the world. By accepting and living according to these two doctrines, we could have joy unspeakable here and eternal happiness hereafter. These are the blessings for which we all should be seeking.

When the lawyer asked Jesus, "Master, which is the great commandment in the law?" Jesus answered: "Thou shalt love the Lord thy God with all thy heart, and with all thy soul, and with all thy mind.

"This is the first and great commandment.

"And the second is like unto it, thou shalt love thy neighbor as thyself" (Matt. 22:36-39).

Let us never forget that the Lord gave us this commandment to love God and to love one another, applying the Golden Rule. We cannot love God without loving our neighbor, and we cannot truly love our neighbor without loving God. This applies to you and to me, and if each of us applies it to himself, we need not worry about the other.

If we are to have this love of which the Savior spoke, and which he emphasizes as being the most important thing in life, it must begin in the home and then carry into our daily lives. Love begins in the home. Sacrifice for one another. Make one another happy.

If there is love between the father and the mother, there will be love between the parents and the children, and among the children. One cannot overemphasize the importance and value of being courteous, kind, considerate, and polite in the home. Where there is true and perfect love in a family, there will be no need to be reminded of such other commandments as "Honour thy father and thy mother," "Thou shalt not steal," "Thou shalt not kill," and "Thou shalt not bear false witness." They will be kept automatically.

By seriously trying to apply the Golden Rule that the Savior gave to us, we will find greater joy, success, satisfaction, and friendship as we go through life, and we will enjoy the love of others, in our friends, in our neighbors, in our wife, in our husband, in our children, they will turn out to be the most wonderful people in the world. On the other hand, if we are looking for their weaknesses and enlarge upon them, these same people may become even despicable.

Sometimes as I move among people I am almost convinced that it is human nature to magnify the weaknesses in others in order to minimize our own. We sing these words in one of our hymns:

> "Let each man learn to know himself;
> To gain that knowledge let him labor,
> Improve those failings in himself
> Which he condemns so in his neighbor.
> How lenient our own faults we view,
> And conscience's voice adeptly smother,
> Yet, oh, how harshly we review
> The selfsame failings in another! . . .
> Example sheds a genial ray
> Of light which men are apt to borrow,
> So first improve yourself today
> And then improve your friends tomorrow."
>   -- Hymns, No. 91

Let us always remember that men of great character need not belittle others or magnify their weaknesses. In fact, the thing that makes them great is the showing of love for and interest in their neighbor's success and welfare. Particularly in discussing religion and politics do we have a tendency to try to tear down another's beliefs and principles. It is distressing to read and hear on every side an attack on an individual who is in public office, whose name is smeared, and whose family suffers also the indignities heaped upon them.

How much better to keep campaigning and debating

on a high plane and to avoid all mud throwing. In fact, people appreciate a campaigner who stands on principle and who avoids personal criticisms. How much better to stand *for* something, not *against* everything.

As we try to apply the Golden Rule, we must realize that love will not permit us to hold grudges or ill feelings. These canker the soul and crowd out love. We hurt ourselves by holding grudges and ill feelings. We hurt and sometimes destroy the person about whom we are bearing tales. We would not think of stealing from or injuring physically one of our associates, friends, or neighbors, but we do even worse by stealing his good name.

It is not uncommon to see people — clerks in stores, secretaries in corporations, individuals in clubs and in affairs in church and state — talking about and criticizing one another, trying to enlarge on their weaknesses with the idea of belittling them in the hope that their own weaknesses might be minimized or overlooked.

Then with love in our hearts for all our neighbors, and with love for our Heavenly Father, we will want to seek first the kingdom of God and his righteousness, knowing that all other things for our good will be added unto us. It has been my observation, wherever I have been in government and in business, that the man who seeks God and his righteousness is happier, more successful, has greater peace of mind, is more highly respected in business, and contributes more to his community and to the happiness and welfare of his family than the man who leaves this out of his life.

I agree with Abraham Lincoln, who said: "God rules this world. I am a full believer that God knows what he wants man to do, that which pleases him. It is never well with that man who heeds it not. Without the assistance of that divine Being I cannot succeed. With it I cannot fail."

Every individual whom I have known, every community in which I have lived, and every country of which I have read, and that I have visited, have convinced me beyond question that where the people accept God and keep his commandments, they are happier, more content, more successful, and more secure. It is the godlessness of people and nations that is causing the unrest so evident in the world today. If only everyone who professes Christianity would apply it in his daily life, we could correct these ills. Let us keep hypocrisy out of our lives and be true Christians.

I believe sincerely that if adults will be honest and true and live the teachings of the gospel and set proper example, we need not worry about our youth. We cannot be satisfied to let any act of ours be responsible for influencing the life of any individual so as to make him wonder or falter or question the truthfulness of the gospel, the plan of life and salvation, and the great sacrifice Jesus made so that we might enjoy eternal life and exaltation. The responsibility is great.

Let us each covenant to seek God and live righteously by keeping his commandments and live in such a way that no one will ever be able to excuse himself because his parents, his adult neighbors, his teachers, or any with whom he might associate, through their actions had given him license or excuse to do anything to bring disastrous results, unhappiness, or failure. And let us so live to be a great influence for good and a light unto the world.

For I am persuaded, that
neither death, nor life, . . .
nor things present, nor
things to come, . . . shall
be able to separate us
from the love of God.

(Romans 8:38, 39)

Chapter Three

A Long Ago Wedding

Clarissa Young Spencer

E arly in November of 1881 Johnnie proposed to me. We had known for many years that sometime we would be married, for we were very much in love. Marriage, we agreed, would be a long way off, for Johnnie had his mother and two sisters to support, and Mother and I were living alone in the big Beehive House. I felt at the time I could never leave mother because the death of my youngest brother Feramorz in September 1881 had so nearly broken her heart.

I shall never forget the night while we were sitting in front of the Franklin Stove in the little downstairs parlor, that we decided to consult mother and ask for her consent to our engagement. I confess to very queer feelings while Johnnie was closeted with mother behind the closed door in the sewing room just back of the southeast front parlor. When he opened the door, he looked so happy that I knew Mother had not only consented to our engagement but had said some lovely things to him.

As we sat together thinking about the future, we heard the door knob softly turn and Mother came into the parlor and sat down, and in her gentle voice said she had been thinking things over and saw no reason for our waiting if John would consent to come to the Beehive House to live. She and I alone in the great big home were lonely without Fera, as we called him, and she went on to say that she felt John, in a measure, would take his place, and she would like us to marry as soon as arrangements could be made. Then she quietly left us in our happiness to talk things over by ourselves. We decided we would be married January 19, 1882.

The following weeks were filled with plans and arrangements. I made my trousseau with the help of my nieces and my sisters Fanny and Talula. My bed linen was made of Fruit of the loom and linen. Mother crocheted the handmade torchon lace and the little fine hemming stitches were hardly visible to the eye.

Long petticoats and nightgowns with embroidery and lace, hand tucked, were pressed, folded and laid in drawers. My wedding dress was made, really not in the style of the 1880's, but I copied it from a dress I had seen an actress wear at the Salt Lake Theatre when I was a little girl. I had never forgotten how beautiful I thought it was. The material was heavy brocaded white satin, and the style was a tight-fitting princess. It was fastened down the back with twenty tiny pearl buttons. Around the waist was a girdle of pearls, and a pocket held by a strand of pearls dropped halfway down onto the skirt. The high collar and three-quarter sleeves were edged with lace that Mother had made. With the help of my sisters I made my dress — but of course, Mother supervised and directed.

The little slippers I wore were size three and one-half, double "A" and were made of the same brocade as the dress. We sent the material back to Philadelphia to Lair Shoeber and Mitchell Co. to have the shoes made.

My stockings were long, heavy-ribbed silk — the first silk stockings I ever had. They looked more like golf apparel than beautiful wedding stockings, but I thought they were lovely.

I wore long white kid gloves — my first ones.

Mother decided that my three ringlets which had been worn down my back should be pinned up into a small bob for my wedding day.

The days passed excitedly and happily. Then came the week before the wedding day. The cooking and the preparation of the food began. The aroma of homemade pies, cakes, doughnuts, and candy filled the house. Hams, tongues, turkeys, chickens were prepared. Mother cooked and cooked. Salad dressings and salads were made. The bottled peaches, pears, and cherries were taken down to the cellar to be chilled for serving.

Talula and I made cakes for three days; white and golden cakes, layer cakes, cream cakes, and sponge cakes. Mother made the doughnuts and mince pies and homemade ice cream. Richard W. Young and Heber J. Grant and George D. Pyper had promised to come and help freeze the ice cream on the day of the wedding.

Aunt Eliza made our beautiful, delicious wedding cake with dozens of fresh eggs and rich milk from the farm. Then Brother Brown, the culliner, came to the Beehive House, and as we all watched, he iced and decorated the tiers of the wedding cake with the pride of an artist. Then he made the cream almonds and peppermints and decorated them. I shall never, never forget the happiness, joy, and excitement of those wonderful days of preparation for Johnnie's and my wedding day.

Our reception was to be held in the Long Hall upstairs. The two Franklin stoves were laid the night before. The long tables where the wedding supper was to be served were set up in the back hall dining room and southeast front sitting room. The linen that Mother had laundered and ironed was as white as snow and looked like satin. The white dishes with the gold bands, and the silverware were in readiness. Before Mother and I retired, we went from room to room to see that all was in order for the important day. How beautiful the Beehive House seemed. To me it was the most wonderful home anyone could ever have.

Early the next morning Mother called, "Clarissa, it is seven o'clock, and you must be at the Endowment House by nine." One of the girls was lighting the fire in the little Franklin stove, and its warmth seemed to calm and steady my nerves as I dressed.

A little after eight Johnnie called for us in a big baroche drawn by a fine span of horses. We drove to the Endowment House and lo and behold, the doors were not opened. We were nearly an hour early!

From my earliest recollection, I had wanted Brother Joseph F. Smith to officiate at my marriage ceremony, and I had long ago received his promise that he would marry us.

After a short wait at the Endowment House, which seemed an eternity to me, Brother Smith came, and we were admitted. Then we dressed and went into the altar room where Brother Smith was waiting. He pronounced a most beautiful blessing on us, his words and the spirit of the occasion have remained with me always and have been a wonderful influence on our marriage and our lives.

After the ceremony we returned to the Beehive House, and in the men's dining room (as we called it), my uncle Feramorz Little was waiting. We sat by the little Franklin stove and then Uncle Feramorz turned to John and me, and in his dear tender way, urged us never to go to sleep at night with any kind of misunderstanding between us. "Talk things over — do not let your troubles grow because of silence. Forgive and then forget." Then he added, "There will be times when you will get very angry but make it a point never to be angry at the same time, and you will find if you obey this rule, your troubles will not last for long."

The hour for our reception approached. When mother and I went up to the southwest room, the room that had been my bedroom all my life, suddenly I began to weep, not because I was not radiantly happy, but I think for the first time, I sensed the full realization that things would never be just the same again; that my girlhood was behind me, and I was overcome with appreciation for my beloved father and mother, my sisters and brothers and their devotion to me and the family life I had had in the Beehive House.

My sisters came up to help me dress, then came my brothers to give their approval and their advice, and in the excitement of the hour, my tears gave way to laughter and happiness.

At last John came up to see me in my wedding dress. My sisters and brothers didn't offer to leave the room as he walked right up to me, took me in his arms, and kissed me. I knew from that moment that I would be safe in his keeping.

He had brought a little bridal bouquet of rosebuds

and white carnations surrounded with lace paper, with the stems wrapped in tinfoil and tied with white baby ribbon.

We went across into the Long Hall and stood in front of the tall mirror at the south end. As I looked at the room with its pale blue walls, coved ceiling, beautiful red brocade drapes, and pretty lace curtains, the carpet with its garlands of roses and leaves, the chandeliers brilliantly lighted with gas, the tall glass lamps on the table and the glowing fires, it seemed that no other room in the whole world could be so beautiful or hold so much joy! I felt that surely I was the most grateful and the happiest bride that ever lived.

The guests numbered three hundred and fifty. As we stood and received congratulations from family and friends, two little flower girls dressed alike in pink China silk dresses, took care that my train was spread out to the best advantage. Mother stood near the doorway to receive, and my brothers and sisters greeted our friends. It was all so lovely to me. The memories of it shall enrich my life always.

The journey of our married life together has been a beautiful one. Children and love have blessed our home. Respect, consideration, and understanding have brought an enrichment throughout the years. Even though we had neither wealth nor greatness as the world recognizes such things, happiness and contentment and blessings have filled our cup of life to overflowing. I am grateful beyond words that on January 19, 1881, Johnnie Spencer chose me as his bride.

Chapter Four

The Test of Love

Richard L. Evans

F or God so loved the world, that he gave his only begotten Son, that whosoever believeth in him should not perish, but have everlasting life" (John 3:16)

It is comfortingly familiar — the love of God simply stated — and what he did about his love is the evidence of it: He sent his Only Begotten Son that whoso believeth in him should have everlasting life.

Suppose God had loved the world in a passive way? Suppose he hadn't sent his Son? Suppose he hadn't given us his gospel? Suppose he hadn't set out to save mankind or redeem us from death? Suppose he had let his children drift without plan or purpose or counsel or commandments? Would that have been love?

An editorial recently read in a medical magazine had an intriguing title: "Love Is a Verb." And from this the writer turned his attention to the importance of doing, of proving, of performing. The proof of any principle is what it does, and the proof of any person is what he does — how he acts, what he becomes — not simply what he says.

"Love Is a Verb."

We might paraphrase and say that service is a verb, that life is a verb; for it is in doing, in living, in learning, and not just in words that we perform our purpose. No one really proves himself or his principles in neutrality or indifference or inaction. No one proves himself by merely thinking or simply sitting.

The writer of this article said that in some primitive languages, with their fewness of words, the description of the movement of game, for example, is described simply by one word: running. Perhaps we could say much more with fewer words by simply indicating the action: living, doing." . . . when a noun replaces a verb there is a disadvantage . . ." because a noun is static, and life is movement. Some people "assign an intrinsic value to 'things' like purity and gratitude . . . They take credit for possessing nominal virtues. Or they punish themselves for having vices, . . . but we communicate with others in verbs . . . Gratitude has not even been born until it has been actually conveyed in word or deed . . ."

Actions do speak louder than words.

As to a young person who was speculating upon whether or not she loved someone, there is the reminder that love is not simply a noun and not simply a sentimental feeling. The proof of love is what one is willing to do for the loved one. The proof of love is how one behaves.

Chapter Five

To A Friend

Grace Stricker Dawson

You entered my life in a casual way,
And saw at a glance what I needed;
There were others who passed me or met me each day,
But never a one of them heeded.
Perhaps you were thinking of other folks more,
Or chance simply seemed to decree it;
I know there were many such chances before,
But the others — well, they didn't see it.
You said just the thing that I wished you would say,
And you made me believe that you meant it;
It held up my head in the old gallant way,
And resolved you should never repent it.
There are times when encouragement means such a lot,
And word is enough to convey it;
There were others who could have as easy as not,
But, just the same, they didn't say it.

There may have been someone who could have done
more
To help me along, though I doubt it;
What I needed was cheering, and always before
They had let me plod onward without it.

You helped to refashion the dream of my heart,
And made me turn eagerly to it;
There were others who might have (I question that part)
—

But, after all, they didn't do it!'

Chapter Six

Love
Unconditional

Marion D. Hanks

I recently had called to my attention an excerpt from Church history that I would like to share with you in part.

"In the latter part of January, 1843, a number of young people assembled at the house of Elder Heber C. Kimball (you realize that the Prophet Joseph Smith is writing this) who warned them against the various temptations to which youth is exposed, and gave an appointment expressly for the young at the house of Elder Billings; and another meeting was held in the ensuing week, at Brother Farr's school-room, which was filled to overflowing. Elder Kimball delivered addresses, exhorting the young people to study the scriptures, and enable themselves to give a reason for the hope within them,' and to be ready to go on to the stage of action, when their present instructors and leaders had gone behind the scenes; also to keep good company and to keep pure and unspotted from the world."

The Prophet then notes that the next meeting was held at his house, and though the weather was inclement, there were many there, to overflowing.

"Elder Kimball," he writes, "as usual, delivered an address, warning his hearers against giving heed to their youthful passions, and exhorting them to be obedient and to pay strict attention to the advice of their parents . . ."

The Prophet then says something that has touched me and I think will touch you who work with youth: "I experienced more embarrassment in standing before them than I should before kings and nobles of the earth; for I knew the crimes of which the latter were guilty, and I knew precisely how to address them; but my young friends were guilty of none of them, and therefore I hardly knew what to say. I advised them to organize themselves into a society for the relief of the poor, and recommended to them a poor lame English brother . . . who wanted a house built, that he might have a home amongst the Saints; that he had gathered a few materials for the purpose, but was unable to use them, and he has petitioned for aid. I advised them to choose a committee to collect funds for this purpose, and perform this charitable act as soon as the weather permitted. I gave them such advice as I deemed was calculated to guide their conduct through life and prepare them for a glorious eternity."

You see, our efforts to reach youth today are not original. They are about the same, motivated with about the same sense of their need, and certainly by the same spirit that directed those of old. This statement of the Prophet moved me because I have had that same feeling when I have stood before them. As a teacher for years, I have pondered their future as I taught them, and I have lived long enough to see the fulfillment of my fondest hopes, or the beginning of the fulfillment of them, for many of them, and, I am sorry to say, the realization of some of my apprehensions. They are, in fact, a great and remarkable generation, yet like many others, I am well aware of the major problems confronting all of our young people, and that many of them desperately need help.

It would be an interesting experience for some of you to walk through a few days of our relationships with youth as we visit with them in person, by telephone, in interviews, by mail. It is just a few days ago that I deplaned at a major airport, met some of your leaders there, and a beautiful young college-age lady who was waiting for me. She had left her home against the wishes of her parents and others and had hitchhiked to a rock festival. On her way home from that adventure, hitch-hiking now with a male companion, she was picked up by officers of the law, arrested for possession of drugs, tried, and sentenced to five years in prison. Through the intervention of our local brethren, who were reached by a distraught mother through the bishop, she was given parole freedom, but the record has been made and her life is hanging in the balance. She has some decisions to make.

On my desk is a letter, one of many, from an anguished girl crying for help. Three times the words are repeated "Please help me." Within hours was a call from a disturbed young man seeking guidance for his friend who questions a Church position which he feels he cannot accept.

In my hand I hold a letter received two days ago from a faithful, broken-hearted father whose son took his own life, notwithstanding the efforts of loving parents and a fine, wholesome family. I wish there were time to read a description of how hard these marvelous parents have tried. This is a missionary family, a committed family, a stay-together family; yet this boy, convinced of his own worthlessness, that he was a failure and that the mistakes he had made were disqualifying, took his own life. His father sent a copy of the note he left, and asked me to make such use of his letter and this letter as judgment and my feelings suggested.

What can we do? How can we help this great young generation meet the challenges of their time? I am certain that we must thoughtfully examine not only their needs and their problems, and what we have to give them, but how we undertake to give it, and what we appear to them to be as they observe it. I have been rethinking my own experience and will give you just an example or two quickly. May I do it in the spirit of a statement that to me for a long time has been very choice: "Neither laugh nor weep, nor loathe, but understand."

What are some of their problems? These basic observations have come from experience with youth and from their own lips and lives. I can sum them up in four or five needs.

First, they need faith. They need to believe. They need to know the doctrines, the commandments, the principles of the gospel. They need to grow in understanding and conviction. They need to worship and to pray, but they live in a time when all of this is so seriously questioned when doubt is encouraged.

Two, they need to be accepted as they are, and to be included. They need a family, the most important social unit in this world; and even if they have a good family, they need the supportive influence outside their home of others, of neighbors, of friends, of bishops, of brothers, of human beings.

Three, they need to be actively involved, to participate, to give service, to give of themselves.

Four, they have to learn somehow that they are more important than their mistakes; that they are worthwhile, valuable, useful; that they are loved unconditionally.

I knelt with my own family, at the conclusion of a great family home evening, the night before our lovely daughter was to be married in the temple. I think she wouldn't mind my telling you that after we had laughed and wept and remembered, she was asked to pray. I don't recall much of her prayer, the tears and the joy and the sweetness, but I remember one thought: she thanked God for the unconditional love she had received. This life doesn't give one very many chances to feel exultant and a little successful, but I felt wonderful that night, and thanked God that she really believes and understands what she said. We cannot, my dear brethren, condition our love by a beard or beads or habits or strange viewpoints. There has to be standards and they must be enforced, but our love must be unconditional.

I'll read you just a sentence from the letter left by the boy who ended his own life: "I have no hope, only dreams that have died. I was never able to obtain satisfactory interpersonal relationships. I feared the future and a lot of other things. I felt inferior. I have almost no will to achieve, perseverance, or sense of worth, so goodbye. I should have listened to you but I didn't. I started using drugs last summer. It's purgatory." What a tragic story!

We need to understand their needs. They need to learn the gospel. They need to be accepted, to be involved; and they need the example of good men, good parents, good people, who really care, and who love unconditionally.

Chapter Seven

Safeguards to a Successful Marriage

C. Douglas Beardall

A glamorous coed with a sorority sticker on her late model sports coupe bashed into a car driven by one of the school's star athletes, resulting in considerable damage to both vehicles. After a heated argument over causes and costs they agreed to meet that evening and try to adjust their differences.

They met that evening, also the following day for lunch, and the next day they were married. They never did adjust their differences. In three months they were divorced.

This is typical of all too many marriages in these days of hurrying and scurrying, "living it up" and rushing in where angels fear to tread. It represents the perfect example of how NOT to go about choosing a life companion.

Should a boy look for his dream girl only when the moon is full as they sit out in their flashy automobile or when she is glamorously attired in her new formal at the senior prom? Should the girl of sweet eighteen look for her "Lochinvar" only when he is sharply dressed for a school function or running for the winning touchdown in the final seconds of the football game? Are there any basic factors that might help young people from plunging into hasty marriage?

Several pertinent suggestions have proved helpful:

1. Don't be in a hurry. Choose a mate over a considerable period of time. To be fair to each other, a couple should take at least six months just to get acquainted and a year after that to prepare for marriage. In making a decision that influences the major portion of a lifetime for you, your companion and possibly several children, isn't it best to take plenty of time to think things over?

2. Understand about love, what it is and what it is not. Many youngsters confuse infatuation with love. Physical attractiveness is only a part of love, not the whole. The love needed for a successful marriage is that feeling of joy and satisfaction in sharing goals, ideals and standards, doing things together and helping each other.

3. Observe the habits and behavior of the prospective partner in various everyday situations. Marriage is jammed with simple, common experiences and oftentimes ugly and annoying situations which are far afield of the soft sophisticated living of today. The more time a couple can spend sharing common, inexpensive, simple and uplifting experiences, the easier it will be to understand each other's behavior after marriage.

4. Find a companion who has much in common with you. Marriage counselors know that the more background factors that are similar, the better the chances a couple has of making a success of marriage. Some of these factors are: race, education, religion and economic and social status.

5. Learn about each other's family. When you marry into a family you marry the whole family whether you like it or not. In-laws can cause a lot of trouble; they can also bring much joy and happiness. It pays to see what they are like.

6. Fast and pray about your decision. Young people are entitled to ask for divine guidance in solving their problems. Certainly, choosing a companion is one of the most important of all decisions. President David O. McKay advised young people: "No couple should ever enter into matrimony without careful observation and serious, prayerful thought."

Marriage is ordained of God and designed to be an eternal relationship. With Latter-day Saints it is not merely a temporal contract effective only on earth during the mortal existence of the parties, but a solemn agreement to extend beyond the grave. This system of holy matrimony involving covenants as to time and eternity, is known as Celestial Marriage and the Church holds the authority, by divine revelation, to so unite couples worthy of this great blessing.

Who can compare such a sacred and holy union with the crash marriage of the college youngsters, married after two days of arguing and divorced after three months?

WE HAVE LIVED AND LOVED TOGETHER

WE HAVE LIVED and loved together
Through many changing years;
We have shared each other's gladness
And wept each other's tears;
I have known ne'er a sorrow
That was long unsoothed by thee;
For thy smiles can make a summer
Where darkness else would be.

Like the leaves that fall around us
In autumn's fading hours,
Are the traitor's smiles, that darken
When the cloud of sorrow lowers;
and though many such we've known, love
Too prone, alas, to range,
We both can speak of one love
Which time can never change.

We have lived and loved together
Through many changing years,
We have shared each other's gladness
And wept each other's tears.
And let us hope the future,
as the past has been will be:
I will share with thee my sorrows,
And thou thy joys with me.

CHARLES JEFFERYS

Chapter Eight

Thou Shalt Love Thy Wife

Henry D. Taylor

After the Lord had created Adam, he made it crystal clear that he did not intend that Adam should go through life without a companion when he said: "It is not good that the man should be alone; I will make him an help-meet for him" (Gen. 2:18). So Eve was created and given to Adam to be his wife and companion.

Many young people in the Church have reached an age where they are old enough to look for a companion and mate. As they commence dating on a steady basis, they will enter a period known as courtship. This will be a thrilling and important time in their lives. President McKay referred to it in these words:

"Courtship is a wonderful period. It should be a sacred one. That is the time in which you choose your mate. Young men, your success in life depends upon that choice. Choose prayerfully the one who inspires you to your best and always remember that no man injures the thing he loves. . . . The seeds of a happy marriage are sown in youth. Happiness does not begin at the altar; it begins during the period of youth and courtship. . . ."

Young people, choose prayerfully and carefully. Don't rush hastily into marriage. Determine that you have common goals and interests. Especially be certain that you possess the same religious convictions and beliefs.

Marriage brings adjustments, because each has his or her own personality. Reared in homes with varying backgrounds, marriage naturally will require the making of adjustments.

Marriage should not be just taken for granted. It must be worked at, but realize that you can have the kind of marriage that you earnestly desire and for which you are willing to work. Marriage will require giving and taking: it will mean sharing, because life was meant to be shared. A happy and successful marriage means forgetting oneself and thinking of ways in which to make one's companion happy. It might be well each day for the husband to think, "What can I do today to make Mary happy:" And Mary should say to herself, "What can I do today to make John happy?" A happy home is where the wife is treated like a queen and the husband is treated like a king. And so, it is not only marrying the right partner, it is being the right partner.

A happy and successful marriage will be one that is built on the important principle of love: a love recognizing not only a fleeting physical attraction, but more importantly a deeply spiritual love that will continue forever. At the dedication of the beautiful Oakland Temple, David O. McKay emphasized the fact that love is eternal in these words: "One great purpose carried out by those who come into the temple is the sealing of man and wife in the sacred bonds of matrimony. That purpose is based upon the fact that man and woman truly love each other. That means that a couple coming to the altar should be sure that there is love in each heart. It would be a terrible thing to be bound for eternity to one whom you do not love, but it is a glorious thing to be sealed for time and eternity to one whom you do love." President McKay then continued, saying, "Let us ever remember that love is the divinest attribute of the human soul . . . love must be fed. . . . love must be nourished; love can be starved to death just as literally as the body can be starved without daily sustenance . . . if that love is fed daily and monthly and yearly through a lifetime, the husband's attention will not be drawn to somebody else . . ." He then concluded with these words: "If your spirit lives after death, as it does, then that attribute of love will persist . . ."

Honeymoons should not end right after the marriage ceremony, but should never cease. President and Sister McKay set a wonderful example to the Church and to the world. On their 65th wedding anniversary President McKay referred to their married life as 65 years of "wedded courtship."

There are many kinds of marriages, but Latter-day Saints should realize that there is only one place on earth where one can obtain a first-class marriage, and that is in a House of the Lord, and it is one of the purposes for which temples are built. What a worthwhile and splendid tradition it is for those who are married and sealed in the temple to return each year on or near their wedding anniversary and recall the promises they have made to each other and to the Lord. This would be in addition to other temple visits.

We are mindful that the Church has constantly stressed the importance of the home. Many valuable and worthwhile suggestions and programs have been introduced to point to ways in which a happy home may be realized.

I am convinced that a happy home is the result of a happy marriage; that is why it is so important to select a suitable companion and mate.

In our world today there is an apparent disregard for the marriage vows made, and we view with concern and alarm the noticeable increase in divorces throughout the land. This would indicate that homes are not happy and, as a result, marriages are failing. Too many men and women become discontented and develop a "roving eye" as their attention is attracted to someone else. Hence, too many divorces are a result of unfaithfulness on the part of the wife, the husband, or both. There would be fewer divorces if the counsel and guidance given by the Lord were followed. In a revelation to the Prophet Joseph he said: "Thou shalt love thy wife with all thy heart, and shalt cleave unto her and none else" (D&C 42:22).

I am persuaded that many divorces today could be avoided and are not justifiable. Stephen L. Richards, a former counselor in the First Presidency, once aptly remarked: "In the case of marital disagreement, which may lead to separation, the proper remedy is not divorce, but repentance — repentance usually on the part of both husband and wife, repentance for both acts committed and harsh words which have made a 'hell' instead of a 'heaven' out of the home."

In order for a married couple to make a "heaven" out of their home, they must realize that repentance, love, faithfulness, humility, and forgiveness are basic essentials in achieving this noble and lofty goal.

A serene home must also be a place where the Spirit of the Lord will dwell and abide. The Spirit of the Lord will not dwell nor abide in a home where there is constant bickering, quarreling, arguing, discord, or disharmony.

The Prophet Joseph had to learn many of these valuable lessons, as we will likewise have to do. David Whitmer, a close associate of the Prophet and one of the Three Witnesses for the Book of Mormon, related an enlightening experience which occurred while the prophet was translating the gold plates. These are Brother Whitmer's words:

"He (Joseph) was a religious and straight-forward man. He had to be: for he was illiterate and could do nothing himself. He had to trust in God. He could not translate unless he was humble and possessed the right feelings towards everyone. To illustrate so you can see: One morning when he was getting ready to continue the translation, something went wrong about the house and he was put out about it — something that Emma, his wife, had done. Oliver and I went upstairs, and Joseph came up soon after to continue the translation but he could not do anything. He could not translate a single syllable. He went downstairs, out into the orchard, and made supplication to the Lord: was gone about an hour — came back to the house, and asked Emma's forgiveness and then came upstairs where we were and then the translation went on all right. He could do nothing save he was humble and faithful."

It is my sincere and humble prayer that we may all live in such a way that we will have happy and serene homes where love abounds and the Spirit of the Lord is ever present.

These things I command you,
that ye love one another.

(John 15:17)

Chapter Nine

Any Wife Or Husband

Carol Haynes

Let us be guests in one another's house
With deferential "no" and courteous "yes";
Let us take care to hide our foolish moods
Behind a certain show of cheerfulness.

Let us avoid all sullen silences;
We should find fresh and sprightly things to say;
I must be fearful lest you find me dull,
And you must dread to bore me any way.

Let us knock gently at each other's heart,
Glad of a chance to look within — and yet
Let us remember that to force one's way
Is the unpardoned breach of etiquette.

So shall I be hostess — you, the host —
Until all need for entertainment ends;
We shall be lovers when the last door shuts,
But what is better still — we shall be friends.

A new commandment I
give unto you, That ye love
one another; as I have
loved you, that ye also
love one another.

(John 13:34.)

Chapter Ten

Expressing Love

Jewel Nelson Beardall

S ome parents came from homes where there were very few expressions of love and too much quarreling. If love is not expressed, usually hostility is. An individual growing up in this kind of environment is inclined to feel self-conscious or embarrassed when he tries to express love. Consequently, even though he may resent his own training, he is inclined to perpetuate the same pattern with his mate and children. The only way such parents can change this pattern is to concentrate every day on expressing love for each other and their children. After a time, the expressions will become easier and more natural.

Another reason for a parent not expressing love for his family is his being so wrapped up in his own life, projects, and problems that he cannot be concerned with the thoughts and feelings of his mate or children. Consequently, they are taken for granted. Some couples are in this situation without realizing it. When the children marry and the parents are left alone, they may no longer find joy in being together. This will not happen to parents who continue through the years to express sincere love for each other in words and actions each day.

Do your children see you as a loving friend in addition to being a disciplinarian? A youth counselor was talking on the phone one day at work. When he had finished, a co-worker said, "I could tell you were talking to a member of your family because you were so firm and authoritative."

Parents are prone to feel that their children know the parents love them regardless of the evidence. A woman who was a devoted mother was shocked by what her five-year old boy revealed. He had suffered a severe hemorrhage following a minor operation. After a week of loving care, he said to his parents, "I've been awfully sick, haven't I? But I'm glad it happened; I didn't know you love me 'till now." He had heard too many negatives and not enough loving approvals.

One young married woman said, "My mother and I will never be close. She told us that she was working because she wanted us to have nice things our father's income would not provide. It's funny, but I can't remember one of those nice things she bought. What I do remember is how unloved I felt, and how miserable and lonely our home was. Even when mother was home, she was too tired or busy to pay any attention to me."

Chapter Eleven

The Vitality Of Love

Milton R. Hunter

T he devil is mustering his forces to full strength to bring about discord, sin, and sorrow among the human family. These calamities can be averted to the extent that people live the basic principle of the gospel of Jesus Christ, which is love.

On a certain occasion a lawyer asked Jesus a question, "tempting him, and saying,

"Master, which is the great commandment in the law?

"Jesus said unto him, Thou shalt love the Lord thy God with all thy heart, and with all they soul, and with all thy mind.

"This is the first and great commandment.

"And the second is like unto it. Thou shalt love thy neighbour as thyself.

"On these two commandments hang all the law and the prophets" (Matt. 22:35-40).

In the days of our Savior, the Hebrew scriptures were divided into divisions. The first five books were called the Law. Another group was called the Prophets. In answering the lawyer, the Master quoted Deuteronomy and Leviticus, which were two of the books of the Hebrew Law. Thus, Jesus Christ was declaring that the two great laws of love were the basis of all the religious teachings of the Hebrew scriptures.

Since the first great commandment is to love the Lord our God, how can we show our love for him? We can show our love in our prayers to the Father, given in the name of the Son, and also through our worship of those divine Beings. But, to become all-inclusive, Jesus said: "If ye love me, keep my commandments" (John 14:15). In other words, we should "live by every word that proceedeth forth from the mouth of God" (D&C 84:44).

Our Eternal Father and his Only Begotton Son both have intense, comprehensive, and full love for us. They have much greater intelligence and understanding than we have, and so their feelings of love go far beyond our capabilities to love. The attribute of love is so highly developed in these Divine Beings that the scriptures state: "God is love" (I John 4:16). In fact, Diety's transcendent love is above and beyond our deepest feelings and keenest conception. At times of great spiritual experience when we feel an abundance of the Spirit, we have a greater realization of the magnitude of God's love.

God is the Father of our spirits. He placed us upon this earth and provided a gospel plan of salvation through his Only Begotten Son, thereby making it possible for us to come back into his presence and receive exaltation or eternal life. Those who attain that glorious condition will experience the sweetness of love, which surpasses our present understanding.

". . . God so loved the world, that he gave his only begotten Son, that whosoever believeth in him should not perish, but have everlasting life" (John 3:16).

Jesus Christ also loved us so much that he freely laid down his life and shed his blood for our sins, and also to bring about a universal resurrection. "Greater love hath no man than this, that man lay down his life for his friends" (John 15:13).

Among the entire human family, there is no example where the principle of love was demonstrated as perfectly as was shown in the life of Jesus in Palestine and in his ministry among the Nephites following his resurrection. He healed the sick, raised the dead, restored sight to the blind, and cleansed those who were afflicted with leprosy. His heart was filled with compassion upon the poor and any who suffered afflictions. He lifted them spiritually with his deep understanding.

A beautiful example of Christ's love and compassion is given in the Book of Mormon when he blessed the little children:

"And when he had said these words, he wept, and the multitude bare record of it, and he took their little children, one by one, and blessed them, and prayed unto the Father for them.

"And when he had done this he wept again;

"And he spake unto the multitude, and said unto them: Behold your little ones.

"And as they looked to behold they cast their eyes towards heaven, and they saw the heavens open, and they saw angels descending out of heaven as it were in the midst of fire; and they came down and encircled those little ones about, and they were encircled about with fire; and the angels did minister unto them" (3 Ne. 17:21-24).

A superb example of Christ's great love is shown when he was hanging on the cross in pain and agony nigh unto death. Jesus prayed: "Father, forgive them; for they know not what they do" (Luke 23:34).

The central theme and the most dynamic force of the gospel of Jesus Christ is love. The Savior taught his apostles:

"A new commandment I give unto you, That ye love one another; as I have loved you, that ye also love one another.

"By this shall all men know that ye are my disciples, if ye have love one to another" (John 13:34-35).

Christ declared that the second great commandment was to love our neighbor as ourselves. The Master Teacher knew that it is human nature for all people to be self-centered. Thus, to be a good Christian, we must love other people as much as we love ourselves. If we loved our neighbors as much as we love ourselves, all our dealings with them would be in kindness, charity, and generosity. All our actions would be tempered by love. Jesus also taught:

"But I say unto you, Love your enemies, bless them that curse you, do good to them that hate you, and pray for them which despitefully use you, and persecute you;

"That ye may be the children of your Father which is in heaven: . . .

"Be ye therefore perfect, even as your Father which is in heaven is perfect" (Matt. 5:44-45, 48).

What should be the relationship between husbands and wives?

A husband and wife should always be gracious and kind to each other. Neither of them should ever say or do anything to hurt the feelings of the other. Deepest love and affection should be shown toward each other continuously. At all times each should make a conscious effort to do everything possible to bring joy and happiness into the life of the other. A husband should show and express appreciation for the accomplishments of his mate, and she should do likewise. We should look for ways to build each other up and make each other happy. Neither the husband nor the wife should let a day pass without expressing love for the other. We should not assume that our mate knows and that it is not necessary to express it. At one time I had the honor of having Joseph Fielding Smith and his beloved wife Jessie attend a conference to which I had been assigned. In her talk Sister Smith said: "I never let a day go by without telling my husband that I love him, and he never lets a day go by without telling me."

Under these circumstances, God's blessings will shower down from heaven upon the married couple and especially for those married by the power of the priesthood in the house of the Lord. The power from on high will bind the love and marriage of such couples for eternity.

David O. McKay, always an advocate of love and harmony in the home, stated: "Homes are made permanent through love."

"Learn the value of self control. You are never sorry for the word unspoken. I believe the lack of self-control is one of the most common contributing factors of unhappiness and discord. We see something in the other which we dislike. It is easy to condemn it. And that condemnatory word arouses ill feeling. If we see it, and we refrain from speaking, in a few moments all is harmony and peace instead of animosity and ill will. Controlling the tongue is one of the greatest contributing factors to happiness in the home, and one which too many of us fail to develop."

Love should also characterize the center of family life. Each child should be made to feel at all times by his parents that he is of great importance in the family. Parents should express their love to their children and show them in numerous ways that they love them dearly. Then the Spirit of the Lord will reside in the home. The family will be love-centered and thereby God-centered. The children in turn will reciprocate the love to the parents and strive to please them.

The goal of families who are actuated deeply by love will be to: keep the commandments of our Savior in every detail and someday come back into the presence of the Eternal Father and his Only Begotten Son to dwell.

Chapter Twelve

Love and Forgive One Another

O. Leslie Stone

I t is an inspiration to all of us to remember the teachings of our Savior and the many wonderful things that he gave to the world. He lived long before recorded history. He was in the great council in heaven — he helped his Father in the shaping of the heavens, in the creation of the earth, and in the making of man.

In opposition to Satan's plan, it was he who proposed man's free agency — giving him the glorious privilege of choice which means so much to all of us.

He lived on earth in the meridian of time — in the promised land.

He went about teaching and doing good. Men followed him, not for worldly riches but to gain treasures in heaven.

He set up a new code for living — to love one another — even one's enemies. He enjoyed us to judge not, to forgive, and to give all men a second chance.

In the Doctrine and Covenants, section 64, verses 8-11, he tells us that it is our duty to forgive one another and that he who does not forgive his brother stands condemned and is the greater sinner.

He gave our society our most undying formula for getting along together when he made this statement found in Matt. 7:12:

"Therefore all things whatsoever ye would that men should do to you, do ye even so to them: for this is the law and the prophets."

There are very few of us that are fully living up to this. Yet I am sure we all agree that if men followed this principle they would solve the problems that we are now facing in all the nations of the earth. Yes, if we lived this principle it would be easy to love and forgive those who trespass against us.

In Matt. 22:36-39, we read about an instance where Christ was approached by some of the leading lawyers of the day who said:

"Master, which is the great commandment in the law? Jesus said unto him, Thou shalt love the Lord thy God with all thy heart, and with all thy soul, and with all thy mind. This is the first and great commandment. And the second is like unto it, Thou shalt love thy neighbor as thyself."

It should be remembered that our nearest neighbors are the members of our own family. Next are those living next door to us, in the same block, the same city, the same state, the nation, yes, even the whole world. All whom we associate with or influence in any way are our neighbors.

Can a man reach the celestial kingdom if he does not love his neighbor as himself? When Jesus gave the second commandment, He said it was like unto the first and repeating both of them he said, "On these two commandments hang all the law and the prophets" (Matt. 22:40).

He made them very important — so important that all other laws and commandments rest upon them.

Let us ask another question. Can a man live the first and great commandment if he does not live the second? In other words, can he love God with all his heart if he does not love his neighbor?

John the apostle said:

"If a man say, I love God, and hateth his brother, he is a liar: for he that loveth not his brother whom he hath seen, how can he love God whom he hath not seen? And this commandment have we from him, That he who loveth God love his brother also" (I John 4:20-21).

In Third Nephi 11:29-30 we find this statement:

"For verily, verily I say unto you, he that hath the spirit of contention is not of me, but is of the devil, who is the father of contention, and he stirreth up the hearts of men to contend with anger, one with another.

"Behold, this is not my doctrine, to stir up the hearts of men with anger, one against another; but this is my doctrine, that such things should be done away."

These statements and many others should make it clear to all of us that the Lord desires us to love and forgive one another. It behooves us to conquer our pride and settle our differences with our fellowmen. As just quoted from Third Nephi, contentions and disputations are of the devil and are not approved by our Heavenly Father. Loving our neighbors as ourselves will bring great joy and happiness into our lives.

Christ practiced forgiveness. You remember the story of the woman that had sinned. The law was that she should be stoned to death. They brought her before the Savior to see how he would judge her. In John 8:6-7 it is recorded:

"This they said, tempting him, that they might have to accuse him. But Jesus stooped down, and with his finger wrote on the ground, as though he heard them not.

"So when they continued asking him, he lifted up himself, and said unto them, He that is without sin among you, let him first cast a stone at her."

Not any in the group could qualify, and the crowd dispersed. He then turned to the woman and said: "Neither do I condemn thee: go, and sin no more" (John 8:11). He certainly did not approve of what she had done, but he demonstrated forgiveness and left it up to his Father in heaven to judge her.

He forgave those who would take his life. At the very time when he was suffering the most, he said: "Father, forgive them; for they know not what they do" (Luke 23:34).

The gospel he brought to earth and which was restored in this dispensation provides us with a beautiful plan of salvation. We know that we had a previous existence and were valiant there. The Lord permitted us to come to earth that we might obtain a body, gain knowledge, develop our skills and our characters, learn to overcome evil, and see if we can remain true and faithful to him, and be sufficiently diligent and obedient to the commandments as to be worthy to return and abide in his presence.

Many of our problems are blessings in disguise. They

are provided so that we might gain the experiences intended for us on this earth and thus prepare us for meeting and solving problems in the next phase of our eternal existence.

Today, as I contemplate the many, many blessings that have been given us, I recall the words of King Benjamin in the Book of Mormon when, after enumerating the blessings which had been poured down upon his people by the Lord, he said this to them: "And behold, all that he requires of you is to keep his commandments" (Mosiah 2:22). Yes, the only thing the Lord requires of us is that we keep his commandments! This sounds relatively simple, doesn't it? But we all know that it isn't simple, nor was it intended to be. Where much is given, much is expected. The Lord requires of those who dwell with him the ability to overcome weaknesses and imperfections. He requires self-denial and self-discipline.

Some of us may feel from time to time that some of the Lord's commandments are an impediment to happiness in this life but this isn't so; and deep down in our hearts we know that so long as we adhere to the commandments, just as surely as night follows day, we will reap the blessings that are promised to the faithful. Sometimes the way of fulfillment may not be apparent to us, but the actuality of it is assured. The Lord said:

"I, the Lord, am bound when ye do what I say; but when ye do not what I say, ye have no promise" (D&C 82:10).

How many of us on judgment day would like to be told that we had failed to do our part — that we had been unworthy servants of the Lord because our own lives had been such a poor example in keeping the commandments?

In Matt. 5:16 the Lord gives us a very important message:

"Let your light so shine before men, that they may see your good works, and glorify your Father which is in heaven."

To fail to keep the commandments of the Lord not only brings condemnation, but actually deprives us of many blessings here on this earth — to say nothing of those eternal blessings for which we are all striving. In I Cor. 2:9 we read this statement:

"Eye hath not seen, nor ear heard, neither have entered into the heart of man, the things which God hath prepared for them that love him."

Think of that great promise. And finally, the wonderful promise given to all men:

"And, if you keep my commandments and endure to the end you shall have eternal life, which gift is the greatest of the gifts of God" (D&C 14:7).

The late President Heber J. Grant told us how to endure to the end when he said:

"Let us do the will of our Father in heaven today — we will then be prepared for the duties of tomorrow and for the eternities to come."

Christ repeatedly emphasized the fact that the gospel is one of work and service. To gain blessings, we must be doers of the word and not hearers only. In Matt. 7:21 we read: "Not every one that saith unto me, Lord, Lord, shall enter into the Kingdom of heaven; but he that doeth the will of my Father which is in heaven."

This means if we are to gain salvation, exaltation, and eternal life we must live in accordance with the principles of the gospel. We must love and forgive all men and keep the commandments of God.

Chapter Thirteen

If You're Ever Going To Love Me

I f you're ever going to love me love me now, while I
    can know
All the sweet and tender feelings which from real affec-
    tion flow.
Love me now, while I am living; do not wait till I am gone
And then chisel it in marble-warm love words on ice-
    cold stone
If you've dear, sweet thoughts about me, why not
    whisper them to me?
Don't you know 'twould make me happy and as glad as
    glad could be?
If you wait till I am sleeping, ne'er to waken here again,
There'll be walls of earth between us and I couldn't hear
    you then.
If you knew someone was thirsting for a drop of water
    sweet
Would you be so slow to bring it? Would you step with
    laggard feet?
There are tender hearts all around us who are thirsting

for our love;
Why withhold from them what nature makes them crave
all else above?
I won't need your kind caresses when the grass grows
o'er my face;
I won't crave your love or kisses in my last low resting
place.
So, then, if you love me any, if it's but a little bit,
Let me know it now while living; I can own and treasure
it.

Chapter Fourteen

The Ultimate Form of Love

Marion D. Hanks

A fter a meeting with a group of students recently, one young man waited to ask a question. "Elder Hanks," he said, "what are YOUR goals? What do YOU want to accomplish?" I observed his seriousness of purpose and answered in the same spirit that my strongest desire is to qualify to be a friend of Christ.

I had not responded to such a question just that way before, but the answer did put into words the deep yearnings of my heart.

In ancient times Abraham was called the "friend of God." Jesus, shortly before his crucifixion, said to his disciples, "Ye are my friends, if ye do whatsoever I command you. Henceforth I call you not servants . . . but I have called you friends" (John 15:14-15).

In 1832 to a group of elders returning from missionary service, he repeated the message: ". . . from henceforth I shall call you friends . . ." (D&C 84:77).

Christ's love was so pure that he gave his life for us:

"Greater love hath no man than this, that a man lay down his life for his friends" (John 15:13). But there was another gift he bestowed while he was on the cross, a gift that further measured the magnitude of his great love: he forgave, and asked his Father to forgive, those who persecuted and crucified him.

Was this act of forgiveness less difficult than sacrificing his mortal life? Was it less a test of his love? I do not know the answer. But I have felt that the ultimate form of love for God and men is forgiveness.

He met the test. What of us? Perhaps we shall not be called upon to give our lives for our friends or our faith (though perhaps some shall), but it is certain that every one of us has and will have occasion to confront the other challenge. What will we do with it? What are we doing with it?

Someone has written: ". . . the withholding of love is the negation of the spirit of Christ, the proof that we never knew him, that for us he lived in vain. It means that he suggested nothing in all our thoughts, that he inspired nothing in all our lives, that we were not once near enough to him to be seizèd with the spell of his compassion for the world."

Christ's example and instructions to his friends are clear. He forgave and he said: ". . . Love your enemies, bless them that curse you, do good to them that hate you, and pray for them which despitefully use you, and persecute you" (Matt. 5:44).

What is our response when we are offended, misunderstood, unfairly or unkindly treated, or sinned against, made an offender for a word, falsely accused, passed over, hurt by those we love, our offerings rejected? Do we resent, become bitter, hold a grudge? Or do we resolve the problem if we can, forgive, and rid ourselves of the burden?

The nature of our response to such situations may well determine the nature and quality of our lives, here and eternally. A courageous friend, her faith refined by many afflictions, said, ". . . Humiliation must come before exaltation."

It is required of us to forgive. Our salvation depends upon it. In a revelation given in 1831 the Lord said:

"My disciples, in days of old, sought occasion against one another and forgave not one another in their hearts; and for this evil they were afflicted and sorely chastened.

"Wherefore, I say unto you, that ye ought to forgive one another: for he that forgiveth not his brother his trespasses standeth condemned before the Lord: for there remaineth in him the greater sin.

"I, the Lord, will forgive whom I will forgive, but of you it is required to forgive all men" (D&C 64:8-10).

Therefore, Jesus taught us to pray. "And forgive us our trespasses as we forgive those who trespass against us" (Matt. 6:14-15).

Does it not seem a supreme impudence to ask and expect God to forgive when we do not forgive? — openly? and "in our hearts"?

The Lord affirms in the Book of Mormon that we bring ourselves under condemnation if we do not forgive (Mosiah 26:30-31).

But not only our eternal salvation depends upon our willingness and capacity to forgive wrongs committed against us, our joy and satisfaction in this life, and our true freedom, depend upon our doing so. When Christ bade us turn the other cheek, walk the second mile, give our cloak to him who takes our coat, was it to be chiefly out of consideration for the bully, the brute, the thief? Or was it to relieve the one aggrieved of the destructive burden that resentment and anger lay upon us?

Paul wrote to the Romans that nothing "shall be able to separate us from the love of God, which is in Christ Jesus our Lord" (Rom. 8:39).

I am sure this is true. I bear testimony that this is true. But it is also true that we can separate ourselves from his spirit. In Isaiah it is written: ". . . your iniquities have separated between you and God . . ." (Isa. 59:2). Again, ". . . they have rewarded evil unto themselves" (Isa. 3:9).

Through Helaman we learn that "whosoever doeth iniquity, doeth it unto himself . . ." (Hel. 14:30): and from Benjamin, ". . . ye do withdraw yourselves from the Spirit of the Lord . . ." (Mosiah 2:36).

In every case of sin this is true. Envy, arrogance, unrighteous dominion — these canker the soul of one who is guilty of them. It is true also if we fail to forgive. Even if it appears that another may be deserving of our resentment or hatred, none of us can afford to pay the price of resenting or hating, because of what it does to us. If we have felt the gnawing, mordant inroads of these emotions, we know the harm we suffer.

So Paul taught the Corinthians that they must "see that none render evil for evil unto any man . . ." (I Thess. 5:15).

It is reported that President Brigham Young once said that he who takes offense when no offense was intended is a fool, and he who takes offense when offense was intended is usually a fool. It was then explained that there are two courses of action to follow when one is bitten by a rattlesnake. One may, in anger, fear, or vengefulness, pursue the creature and kill it. Or he may make full haste to get the venom out of his system. If we pursue the latter course we will likely survive, but if we attempt to follow the former, we may not be around long enough to finish it.

Years ago on Temple Square I heard a boy pour out the anguish of his troubled heart and make a commitment to God. He had been living in a spirit of hatred toward a man who had criminally taken the life of his father. Nearly bereft of his senses with grief, he had been overcome with bitterness.

On that Sabbath morning when others and I heard him, he had been touched by the Spirit of the Lord, and in that hour through the pouring in of that spirit had flooded out the hostility that had filled his heart. He tearfully declared his determined intent to leave vengeance to the Lord and justice to the law. He would no longer hate the one who had caused the grievous loss. He would forgive and would not for another hour permit the corrosive spirit of vengefulness to fill his heart.

Sometime later, touched with the remembrance of that moving Sabbath morning, I told the story to a group of people in another city. Before I left that small community the next day I had a visit from a man who had heard the message and understood it. Later a letter came from him. He had gone home that night and prayed and prepared himself and had then made a visit to the place of a man in his community who had years before imposed upon the sanctity of his home. There had been animosity and revenge in his heart and threats made. That evening when it was made known that he was at the door, his frightened neighbor appeared with a weapon in his hand. The man quickly explained the reasons for his visit, that he had come to say he was sorry, that he did not want hatred to continue to consume his life. He offered forgiveness and sought forgiveness and went his way in tears, a free man for the first time in years. He left a former adversary also in tears, shaken and repentant.

The next day the same man went to the home of a relative in the town. He said, "I came to ask your forgiveness. I don't remember why we have been so long angry, but I have come to tell you that I am sorry and to beg your pardon and to say that I have learned how foolish I have been." He was invited in to join the family at their table, and was reunited with his kin.

When I heard his story I knew again the importance of qualifying ourselves for the forgiveness of Christ by forgiving.

Robert Louis Stevenson wrote: "The truth of Christ's teaching seems to be this: In our own person and fortune, we should be ready to accept and pardon all. It is our cheek we are to turn and our coat we are to give to the man who has taken our cloak. But when another's face is buffeted, perhaps a little of the lion will become us best. That we are to suffer others to be injured and stand by, is not conceivable and surely not desirable."

So there are times when, in defense of others and principle, we must act. But of ourselves, if we suffer injury or unkindness, we must pray for the strength to forebear.

Christ gave his life on a cross: and on that cross he fully, freely forgave. It is a worthy goal to seek to qualify for the friendship of such a one.

More than 250 years ago Joseph Addison printed in The Spectator a paragraph of sobering thoughtfulness:

"When I look upon the tombs of the great, every emotion of envy dies in me; when I read the epitaphs of the beautiful, every inordinate desire goes out; when I meet with the grief of parents upon a tombstone, my heart melts with compassion; when I see the tombs of the parents themselves, I consider the vanity of grieving for those whom we must quickly follow; when I see kings lying by those who deposed them, when I consider rival wits placed side by side, or the men that divided the world with their contests and disputes, I reflect with sorrow and astonishment on the little competitions, factions, and debates of mankind. When I read the several dates of the tombs, of some that died yesterday, and some six hundred years ago, I consider that great Day when we shall all of us be contemporaries, and make our appearance together."

God help us to rid ourselves of resentment and pettiness and foolish pride; to love and to forgive in order that we may be friends with ourselves, with others, and with the Lord.

"Even as Christ forgave you, so also do ye" (Col. 3:13).

See that ye love one another
with a pure heart fervently.
(1 Peter 1:22)

Chapter Fifteen

The Power Of Love

Jewel Nelson Beardall

D o you wonder why love and the ability to get along with others has such power? Do you wonder why it is that, unless you are able to get along with others in either a business way or at home, all your other training, abilities and efforts are generally futile?

The Bible asserts that love never fails. (I John 4:16) Jesus pointed out to the lawyer that love fulfills the whole law, (Matt. 22:40) meaning the whole law of healthy, happy, harmonious, successful living. Love has unequaled power, because love is the power that unifies the whole world and everything in it. Love is the equalizing, harmonizing, balancing, adjusting force that is ever at work throughout the universe. Working in these ways, love can do for you what you cannot humanly do for yourself.

At Harvard University, world-renowned sociologists conducted research studies on the power of love. The university established a research center, staffed with

serious scientists, who spent their valuable time study-
ing the subject of love. Their findings were that love, like
other good things, can be deliberately produced by
human beings! According to their findings, there is no
reason why we can't learn to generate love as we do
other natural forces.

If you will analyze this miracle called love, you will
discover that life is a process of giving and receiving of
love in its many phases, and that it is those individuals
who are not living in the stream of love that feel its lack as
a difficulty in mind, body or affairs. Through the deliber-
ate development of love, you can get into the stream of
life's goodness, as well as help others to experience it.

Is it not wonderful to realize, as did the Harvard
scientists, that you no longer have to look outside yourself, waiting and hoping that somehow, at some future
time, perhaps love will find you? You can begin now
deliberately generating love for God, for yourself and for
mankind, from within your own being. By doing so, you
will unfailingly draw the perfect expressions of love into
your own life.

I have discovered that some people feel guilty about
their desire for love in its many phases, thinking they
should suppress that desire. The time has come for you
to realize that you should express the desire for love-
from within out, toward Heavenly Father, yourself, and
your fellow man. It is through your own thoughts, feelings and expectations that love is born. As you deliberately express love, it comes back to you multiplied.

Take conscious control of your thoughts and feelings,
and begin now to develop a consciousness of love,
knowing that it is the quickest way to solve your own
problems, as well as a powerful way of helping mankind.
You can do this in a very simple way:

Begin spending a few minutes each day deliberately generating love. In those times affirm: With the Lord's help, I am now deliberately and joyously radiating divine love to myself, to my family, and to all mankind. Ask daily that love be made alive in you. Form the mental picture of yourself as healthy, prosperous, illumined, harmonized, blessed, unfettered and unbound.

In these periods when you deliberately bring alive and generate love, do so in this way: Think of love as being a radiant light that enfolds, brightens, illumines and uplifts you. Think of love as permeating, penetrating, and saturating your whole being. If there are dark, troublesome areas in your life, deliberately think of them as coming alive with the light of love and being divinely adjusted.

Continue in your meditation period to pour forth the thought, feeling, and enlightened picture of love upon yourself and your world. There is no reason for feeling guilty about loving yourself. You cannot love others or radiate love outward until you love yourself and feel it within. Love begins at home, within you. Psychiatry emphasizes the need for self-love and appreciation. When Jesus said, Love the Lord thy God with all they heart . . . soul . . . and mind. This is the great and first commandment, (Matt. 22:35) He was referring to man's loving himself, as well as God.

Dare to consciously love yourself, love your life and affairs, love every little bit of good in all. Dare to direct love to any situation in your life that seems difficult.

When you have sufficiently gained a mental picture and satisfying feeling of the light of love flooding your whole being, you can know that you have generated and released the greatest power on earth into every phase of your mind, body and affairs. The light of love shall shine forth as new energy, new peace of mind, new power and dominion, new poise, new beauty, new prosperity, new harmony; indeed, as new good in every phase of your life.

We have mentioned a number of ways to generate and radiate love in the impersonal phases of life, but let us not overlook the fact that the personal aspects of love need to be expressed regularly in every family. Psychologists tell us that everyone needs to feel loved, appreciated and important; it is a basic need of all mankind. Often those troublesome situations at home, in the family group, result from lack of love being expressed on a personal basis.

For instance, I recently asked a lady who was having trouble in her marriage, "When was the last time you looked your husband straight in the eye and sincerely declared to him, 'I love you and I think you're wonderful!' Startled, she replied, "You mean I have to talk like that to save my marriage?" I found myself saying, "Well, isn't that the way you got your husband in the first place?"

The sexual relationship in marriage is also an important way of expressing love. Indeed, when rightly understood, sex is a vital part of the holy covenant of marriage. In its fullest meaning, sex is beautiful beyond compare. The expression of sex in marriage can deeply enhance the bond of love.

Children, as well as adults, need to feel wanted and appreciated. Recently a seventh grade school teacher made an interesting experiment with the 12 and 13 year-old students in her classes. She gave the boys and girls slips of paper on which she asked them anonymously to write out their greatest problems in life. She read most of their answers to me.

One student revealed that:

> My mother and father give me everything I
> want in the way of clothes, money and gifts. But
> they never have time to talk or visit with me. My
> friends say that I am very lucky to have such
> generous parents. But I would much rather
> have more of their time and less of their money.

In counseling parents about their so-called "problem
children," one quickly discovers that often the parent's
attitude toward the child is the problem. A change of
attitude on the part of the parent toward the child is often
all that is needed to bring about a happy relationship. In
recent conversation, a very successful businessman
seemed quite troubled about his non-conformist teen-
age son. This man had two sons, one of whom had
grown up to be all that his father had desired as a loving,
obedient individual. The other son had simply refused to
be molded to his father's opinion of the type of person he
should be.

This younger son possessed a highly creative nature,
and was interested in the world of art, music and writing. However, the father had condemned these artistic
talents in his son, rather than recognizing that they were
God-given. When the father realized that there was nothing "wrong" with this son, that he was simply a different type from the older son or from anyone else in the
family, the father seemed relieved and agreed to praise
his son's creative abilities. Later he encouraged his
young son to take the art courses he had always wanted.

Children, as well as adults, especially thrive on sincere appreciation, praise and encouragement; it is a tonic
to them. I know of an instance of a little boy who was not

responding in school at all. His mother became disgusted with him and made an appointment with a psychiatrist, which was scheduled some weeks later. In casual conversation she mentioned her son to me, and I pointed out his sensitivity and his creative abilities. I explained that his differentness, which had so greatly disturbed her, was his potential power of success. I suggested that she take time from her crowded business schedule to daily sit down and talk with him about anything that was on his mind, and especially that she praise his every improvement and his every good attitude.

She immediately began praising him sincerely and daily, and his schoolwork immediately responded. His musical ability also blossomed forth. Soon he was selected as one of six children in his age group from the entire city to perform at a special band concert. The previously planned psychiatric treatment was cancelled.

This does not mean you should not work to correct negative behavior or to discipline children. You should be firm but loving in your discipline. The word discipline in its root meaning signifies "to perfect." Your methods of correction and discipline should lead to perfection rather than to rebellion, resistance, or further negative behavior. I have found it best to pray for divine guidance concerning each child, rather than to seek advice from other people, or to clutter the mind with too much theory on the subject.

Parents have long believed that they personally had the difficult task of training their children by ingrafting knowledge onto them from the outside, which they felt would equip their children for adult living. When you attempt to rear children from this standpoint alone, it can prove difficult and disappointing for all concerned.

Intellectual education has its place, but it is only a part

of a child's real education and development. The word "educate" truly means to "draw out" that which innately exists within.

Another way to love children is to teach them that Heavenly Father never intended them to fail or to be in lack. I know of one family in which the children are developing real self-confidence because their parents constantly tell them they can succeed, and that failure is not necessary. These children are always gathered together at bedtime for their prayers.

Remember that love functions on both the personal and impersonal phases of life. If there seems to be a lack of love in your personal life, you can be assured that you will experience love in that department, when you persevere in rendering love impersonally as service and good will. If love seems to be missing in the impersonal phases of your life, you can be assured that you will experience understanding, happiness and success there, when you persevere in using the Lord's love in your personal life and relationships.

Charles Fillmore commented on the power of love as follows:

> You may trust love to get you out of your difficulties. There is nothing too hard for it to accomplish for you, if you put your confidence in it.

Serious scientists have made a special study of love. Jesus Christ, the Master of victorious living, placed it first in importance. One of the early builders of Christianity, the Apostle Paul, ascribed all power to it.

Promise yourself now that you will also begin to deliberately generate Heavenly Father's love to yourself,

your family, and to all mankind. As you do, your problems will turn into solutions, and your blessings will
multiply.

Chapter Sixteen

Our Precious Families

Loren C. Dunn

T he family — mother and father and the children — is the oldest of all our institutions and stands at the very foundation of our civilization. There can be nothing more precious or enduring than the family. It is obvious that the need exists, however, for the upgrading of the role of parents in the family setting.

I remember a few years ago going on a business trip to eastern Canada in company with a broad range of business and community leaders. After the business of the day, we had dinner together; and during the course of the evening, as everyone began to relax and get better acquainted, one of those present, for no apparent reason, began to tell about his son, a boy whom obviously he loved very much. Yet there was conflict and even some alienation and he wasn't quite sure what to do, if indeed he should do anything.

That comment prompted a similar response from the others seated around the table. You could tell it was something they were not used to talking about, but each was personally concerned about some aspect of his family life, and this was primarily associated with his children.

Although we live in an era of transition and change, I believe parents are as anxious and concerned about their children as they have ever been. If the family, then, is the foundation unit in society, perhaps there is need to reaffirm some basic principles.

First, that parents recognize they have the right to structure the attitudes and conduct of their children, not only the right but the responsibility.

Second, that the principle of work, the work ethic if you please, be taught by the parents in the family setting. Where else is the dignity of work to be taught if not in the home?

And, third, parents have a right to establish the moral and spiritual tone in the family to help family members to realize the importance of living divine principles as a means of accomplishment and of peace of mind.

First, then, the right of parents to structure the attitudes and conduct of their children. Fundamentally, this is a divine right. God says of Abraham that he "shall surely become a great and mighty nation . . . for I know him, that he will command his children and his household after him, and they shall keep the way of the Lord to do justice and judgment" (Gen. 18:18-19). God could make Abraham head of a numerous posterity because of his faithfulness in teaching his children.

There are some in the world who might say that such parental influence is repressive and robs the child of its freedom, but quite the opposite is true. A group of young girls was overheard talking about the parents of one of their friends. Showing maturity beyond her years, one of the girls said, "Her parents don't love her; they let her do anything she wants." The others agreed.

In a New York Times Magazine article, later condensed in Reader's Digest, William Shannon makes the following points: "American children . . . are suffering from widespread parent failure. By their words and actions (he says) many fathers and mothers make it clear that they are almost paralyzed by uncertainty . . . Many parents are in conflict as to what their own values are. Others think they know, but lack the confidence to impose discipline in behalf of their values.

What is lacking, he says, is not more information on child development, but conviction. Although heredity plays some role in the development of a child, the greater influence "depends on whether parents care enough about their children to assert and defend the necessary values." The author also says that both mother and father need to put family and home responsibilities first. "Rearing our children is by far the most important task that most of us will ever undertake."

He also states that "parents who do not persevere in rearing their children according to their own convictions are not leaving them 'free' to develop on their own. Instead, they are letting other children and the media, principally television and the movies, do the job."

The greatest principle to be learned in the family setting is love. If parents will influence and direct and persevere with love, then members of the family will also make that principle a part of all they do. The principle of love can overcome many parental mistakes in the raising of their children. But love should not be confused with lack of conviction.

Secondly, that the principle of work be taught in the family and home setting. There is evidence to support that at least in the United States the problems of stress and tension might be linked to a gradually decreasing average number of hours worked by the labor force. The suggestion is that free time, not work, might be a major cause of stress and tension in individuals.

While we were growing up in a small community, my father saw the need for my brother and me to learn the principle of work. As a result, he put us to work on a small farm on the edge of town where he had been raised. He ran the local newspaper, so he could not spend much time with us except early in the morning and in the evening. That was quite a responsibility for two young teenagers, and sometimes we made mistakes.

Our small farm was surrounded by other farms, and one of the farmers went in to see my father one day to tell him the things he thought we were doing wrong. My father listened to him carefully and then said, "Jim, you don't understand. You see, I'm raising boys, and not cows." In spite of the mistakes, we learned how to work on that little farm, and I guess, although they didn't say it in so many words, we always knew we were more important to Mother and Father than the cows or, for that matter, anything else.

Certainly in every home all family members can be given responsibilities that will fall within their ability to accomplish and, at the same time, teach them the satisfaction and dignity of work.

The third point is that parents have the right to teach moral and spiritual principles to their children. In that regard let me quote the following from modern scripture:

"And again, inasmuch as parents have children in

Zion, or in any of her stakes which are organized, that teach them not to understand the doctrine of repentance, faith in Christ the Son of the living God, and of baptism and the gift of the Holy Ghost by the laying on of the hands, when eight years old, the sin be upon the heads of the parents" (D&C 68:25).

In his first address to the United States Congress, President Gerald Ford stated this universal truth: "If we can make effective . . . use of the moral and ethical wisdom of the centuries in today's complex society, we will prevent more crime and corruption than all the policemen and prosecutors . . . can ever deter." And he added: "This is a job that must begin at home, not in Washington."

In the article previously mentioned, Mr. Shannon says, "Nothing has invalidated the hard-earned moral wisdom that mankind has accumulated since Biblical times. To kill, to steal, to lie, or to covet another person's possessions still leads to varying degrees of misery for the victim and the perpetrator . . . 'Thou shalt not commit adultery' may sound old-fashioned, but restated in contemporary terms — 'Do not smash up another person's family life' — still carries a worthwhile message."

He also points out the virtues of self-denial and anticipation. As older teenagers learn the facts about sex, it would do no harm, he says, to use self-control.

"A certain amount of frustration and tension can be endured — and with good effect. Only modern Americans," he says, "regard frustration as ranking higher than cholera in the scale of human afflictions."

These are but three of many principles that should be emphasized in the setting of family and home.

WILL YOU LOVE ME WHEN I'M OLD?

I WOULD ASK of you, my darling,
   A question soft and low,
That gives me many a heartache
   As the moments come and go.

Your love I know is truthful,
   But the truest love grows cold;
It is this that I would ask you:
   Will you love me when I'm old?

Life's morn will soon be waning,
   And its evening bells be tolled,
But my heart shall know no sadness,
   If you'll love me when I'm old.

Down the stream of life together
   We are sailing side by side,
Hoping some bright day to anchor
   Safe beyond the surging tide.
Today our sky is cloudless,
   But the night may clouds unfold;
But, though storms may gather round us,
   Will you love me when I'm old?

When my hair shall shade the snowdrift,
   And mine eyes shall dimmer grow,
I would lean upon some loved one,
   Through the valley as I go.
I would claim of you a promise,
   Worth to me a world of gold;
It is only this, my darling,
   That you'll love me when I'm old.

Chapter Seventeen

Love, Courtship And Marriage

David O. McKay

I n courtship and marriage we can modify and control to a very great extent our environment. How important it is, then, that the companion of each be chosen wisely and prayerfully. The choosing of a companion determines our future happiness or unhappiness. It is a part of wisdom, therefore, to associate only with those from whose company you select a life's partner with whom you will be congenial. If in such companionship you recognize negative characteristics in the person who attracts you, try to let your judgment rule your heart. Don't fool yourselves by thinking that by marriage a person will overcome evil habits or negative traits of character. Let these be proved before marriage.

What are the positive characteristics for which we should seek? Among the dominant characteristics a true lover should possess are honesty, loyalty, chastity, and reverence. Never marry anyone who would deceive you, who would tell you a lie. The real guiding principle, however, is the divinest attribute of the soul — love.

Young men and women have just entered into that state of life when they are driven by heaven-bestowed passions — I say God-given passions. There are young persons who, recognizing this fact, say: "Having them, why cannot we gratify them?" And they receive justification sometimes from modern psychologists. But do not be misled. I repeat, you are at that period of life in which your physical nature manifests itself, but you must also remember that God has given you, in that same period of life, powers of reasoning; he has given you judgment, and these for a divine purpose. Let reason and judgment be your guide — your balance.

Did you ever stand by the side of a power engine — throbbing, throbbing, throwing out its power and disseminating heat? On those stationary engines, you will find balances. If it were not for them, the whole building might be blown up. But as the heat intensifies, those balances are thrown farther out and out, so that the whole thing is under control. So you have your reason, your judgment as balances to your passion. Try not to lose these balances, or there may be an explosion that will wreck your life.

To look upon marriage as a mere contract that may be entered into at pleasure in response to a romantic whim, or for selfish purposes, and severed at the first difficulty or misunderstanding that may arise, is an evil meriting severe condemnation, especially in cases wherein children are made to suffer because of separation.

The seeds of a happy married life are sown in youth. Happiness does not begin at the altar; it begins during the period of youth and courtship. Selfmastery during youth and the compliance with the single standard of morality is first, the source of virile manhood; second, the crown of beautiful womanhood; third, the foundation of a happy home; and fourth, the contributing factor to the strength and perpetuity of the race!

I sincerely believe that too many couples come to the marriage altar looking upon the ceremony as the end of courtship.

Let all the members of the Church look upon that ceremony as the beginning of an eternal courtship. Let us not forget that during the burdens of home life tender words of appreciation and courteous acts are even more appreciated than during those sweet days and months of courtship.

It is after the ceremony and during the trials that daily arise in the home that a word of *thank you, pardon me, if you please,* contributes to the perpetuation of that love which brought you to the altar.

Keep in mind three great ideals that contribute to happiness after the marriage ceremony.

First, *loyalty*. You have no right, young man, to yield to the attention of any young woman other than that sweet wife, and you, husband, have no right even to attract the attention of another man's wife. Her duty is with her husband, building a home. Loyalty to the great covenant made at that altar!

Second, *self-control*. Little things annoy, and you speak quickly, sharply, loudly, and wound the other's heart. I know of no virtue that helps to contribute to the happiness and peace of a home more than the great quality of self-control in speech. Refrain from saying the sharp word that comes to your mind at once if you are wounded or if you see something in the other that offends you. In a few minutes you will be glad that you did not say the harsh word, that you did not commit the impulsive act, and the result is love and peace in the home.

The third ideal is that little simple virtue of *courtesy* —
parents courteous to their children and children courteous to father and mother, and there is an element of
refinement in the home. *Loyalty, self-control, courtesy.*

Fifteen years, thirty years, fifty years, and throughout eternity — be just as courteous to each other as you
were when you courted. It makes a happy home. I know
of no other place where happiness abides more surely
than in the home. It is possible to make home a bit of
heaven. Indeed, I picture heaven as a continuation of the
ideal home.

Chapter Eighteen

Love And Marriage

Hugh B. Brown

Marriage is and should be a sacrament. The word *sacrament* is variously defined, but among Christian people it signifies a religious act or ceremony, solemnized by one having proper authority. It is a pledge, or solemn covenant, a spiritual sign or bond between the contracting parties themselves and between them and God. That marriage was instituted and sanctified by the Lord himself is shown by the following quotations: "And the Lord God said, it is not good that the man should be alone; I will make him an help meet for him.

"Therefore shall a man leave his father and his mother, and shall cleave unto his wife: and they shall be one flesh." (Genesis 2:18, 24.)

When Jesus departed from Galilee and came into the coasts of Judea beyond Jordan, a great multitude followed him, and the Pharisees questioned him regarding divorce: "And he answered and said unto them, Have ye not read, that he which made them at the beginning made them male and female.

"And said, For this cause shall a man leave father and mother, and shall cleave to his wife: and they twain shall be one flesh.

"Wherefore they are no more twain, but one flesh. What therefore God hath joined together, let not man put asunder." (Matthew 19:4-6)

It is plain that God intended that man and woman should become one. By personally officiating at this wedding he sanctified the institution of marriage. It is a normal, healthful, and desirable state and was instituted to fulfil God's purpose in the earth.

It is the central element in the domestic establishment. It is more than a human institution to be regulated solely by custom and civil law. It is more than a contract under the sanction of moral law. It is or should be a religious sacrament by which men and women solemnly undertake to co-operate with God in his avowed purpose to make earth life and mortality available to his spirit children and to bring to pass their immortality and eternal life.

There are those who say that the highest, most dedicated, and most desirable life may be achieved outside the marriage covenant. In other words they would forbid those who seek the highest glory to be "contaminated by physical and animal-like associations." There is no warrant in the scripture for such doctrine. In the book of Proverbs we read: "Whoso findeth a wife findeth a good thing, and obtaineth favour of the Lord." (Proverbs 18:22) And the Apostle Paul in writing to Timothy, said: "Now the Spirit speaketh expressly, that in the latter times some shall depart from the faith, giving heed to seducing spirits, and doctrines of devils,

"Speaking lies in hypocrisy; having their conscience seared with a hot iron;

"Forbidding to marry, and commanding to abstain from meats, which God hath created to be received with thanksgiving of them which believe and know the truth." (1 Timothy 4:1-3, italics added.) And in the Doctrine and Covenants we read: "And again, verily I say unto you, that whoso forbiddeth to marry is not ordained of God, for marriage is ordained of God unto man." (D&C 49:15)

The Latter-day Saints believe that in order to attain the best in life and the greatest happiness in this world and for the next, men and women must be married in the temple for time and eternity. Without the sealing ordinances of temple marriage, man cannot achieve a godlike stature or receive a fulness of joy because the unmarried person is not a whole person, is not complete.

To a Latter-day Saint there is only one kind of marriage which is wholly acceptable, that is temple or celestial marriage, which is performed only in the temples of the Church. Temples are erected and dedicated in holiness to the Lord to provide a place where spiritual and eternal ceremonies and ordinances may be performed. While we recognize civil marriages performed by ministers of other churches, and civil marriages performed by officers of the law, or others legally qualified to perform them, we believe that only in a temple of God can a marriage for time and eternity be performed, and then only by one having the authority which Christ gave to Peter when he said: ". . . whatsoever thou shalt bind on earth shall be bound in heaven: . . ." (Matthew 16:19)

This authority is referred to in the scriptures as "the keys of the kingdom of heaven," *(idem)* and in celestial marriage those keys open the door to that kingdom.

Man has certain basic needs — moral, social, biological, and spiritual — and these can only be fully realized in the God-ordained institution of eternal marriage.

To live the abundant life here and eternal life hereafter, man must love and be loved, serve and sacrifice, have responsibility and exercise his God-given creative powers. ". . . I am come that they might have life, and that they might have it more abundantly." (John 10:10)

But perhaps the greatest value of marriage is not that which accrues to the individual man and woman. The purpose of their union in the beginning is indicated by the Lord's commandment, "Be fruitful, and multiply, and replenish the earth, and subdue it: . . ." (Genesis 1:28) In proper marriage there is opportunity for man to realize his natural urge to be creative and productive. This can be completely fulfilled and properly enjoyed only in the marriage relationship, in child bearing and child rearing. Parents should remember that the children born to them — their children — are also the children of God. He is the Father of their spirit bodies, and during the pre-earth existence he wisely made provision for eternal element and eternal spirit to be inseparably connected and receive a fulness of joy. Latter-day Saints therefore believe that God is actually the third partner in this relationship and that bringing children into the world within the divinely sanctioned institution of marriage is part of his plan to bring to pass the immortality and eternal life of man.

When the Lord Jesus designated love of God and love of fellow men as the two great commandments he glorified love. In fact, we are told that God is love. Therefore as God is eternal, so love must be eternal, and its fruits and blessings are intended to continue throughout the eternities to come. But to enjoy the privileges and advantages of eternal love as it relates to husbands and wives, parents and children, the ordinance which authorizes and sanctifies this most beautiful of all relationships is not acceptable, if it contains the limitation "until death do you part." For family relationship and conjugal associations to be eternal, the marriage contract must *authoritatively* state, "for time and for all eternity."

All people should realize their responsibility to their offspring and to the covenants they make with respect thereto. When the Lord said, "We without them cannot be made perfect" (D&C 128:18), he was referring to a chain whose links extend into the future as well as the past. In fact, we may have more direct responsibility for those entrusted to us in this life than to our ancestors. We cannot be held responsible for the sins, either of commission or of omission of our ancestors, but he has warned that in case of failure on the part of our posterity, if it can be attributed to our failure in our duty to them, then the sins will be upon our heads.

Among the blessings of those who attain the highest degree in the celestial kingdom is the blessing of eternal increase, which, among other things, means that even after death men may continue to co-operate with God in bringing to pass the immortality and eternal life of man.

The Latter-day Saint concept of eternal progression includes eternal development, eternal increase of knowledge, power, intelligence, awareness, and all the characteristics and capacities which make for Godhood. But in the economy of God men cannot attain this state of continuing perfection in his unfinished or unmarried state. There must be growth and increase of the whole man, in other words, the man who has found and been united to his other half.

This concept of marriage, with its divine perspective, gives new meaning and adds importance, dignity, and glory to the idea of marriage. With this concept the thoughtful person will be more careful and selective in the choice of his eternal companion. Certainly before entering into such an eternal contract both men and women should be humble and thoughtful and should prayerfully seek for divine guidance.

The religious sanctity and sanction of the marriage relationship is greatly enhanced and appreciated where the couple, before marriage — and they must, necessarily, be of the same faith — start with the same goal in mind. They must prepare and be worthy to receive the sacred ordinance in edifices where only the worthy may enter. Here they receive instruction, make covenants, and then at the altar pledge eternal love and fidelity, each for the other, in the presence of God and of angels. Surely such a concept and practice, with its accompanying obligations, makes for the permanence of the home, the glorifying of the institution of marriage, and the salvation of the souls of men.

Such marriage is essentially an act of faith, solemnized in the presence of a divine partner. There must be faith and courage to see it through, to endure to the end, despite the difficulties, trials, disappointments, and occasional bereavements.

When one accepts the conditions and obligations of this eternal partnership, he must realize that failure here is almost total failure. Whatever his successes may be in other fields of activity, if a man fails to discharge the obligations imposed by the eternal covenant, the appalling penalty will be the loss of celestial glory, accompanied by responsibility for the losses sustained by those with whom he made the contract and for whom he is responsible.

". . . marriage is ordained of God unto man.

"Wherefore, it is lawful that he should have one wife, and they twain shall be one flesh, and all this that the earth might answer the end of its creation;

"And that it might be filled with the measure of man, according to his creation before the world was made." (*Ibid.*, 49:15-17)

And this I pray, that your
love may abound.

(Philippians 1:9)

Chapter Nineteen

Johnny Lingo And The Eight-Cow Wife

Patricia McGerr

W hen I went to the islands, I took along a notebook. I had a three-week leave between assignments in Japan, so I borrowed a boat and sailed to Kiniwata. The notebook was supposed to set me on the path to becoming a junior-grade Maugham or Michener. When I got back it was half filled, mostly with descriptions of flora and fauna, native customs and costumes. But the only sentence among all the notes that still interests me is the one that says: Johnny Lingo gave eight cows to Sarita's father. And I don't need to have that in writing. I'm reminded of it every time I see a woman belittling her husband or a wife withering under her husband's scorn. I want to go up and say to them, "You should know why Johnny Lingo paid eight cows for his wife." But of course I don't say anything. I only think about it.

Johnny Lingo wasn't exactly his name. But I wrote it down that way because I learned about the eight cows

from Shenkin, the fat manager of the guest house at
Kiniwata. He was from Chicago and had a habit of
Americanizing the names of the islanders. I guess it
made him feel more at home. He wasn't the only one
who talked about Johnny Lingo, though. He was mentioned by many people in many connections. If I wanted
to spend a few days on the island of Nurabandi, a day's
sail away, Johnny Lingo could put me up, they told me,
since he had built (unheard-of luxury!) a five-room
house. If I wanted fresh vegetables, his garden was the
greenest. If it was pearls I sought, his middlemanship
would bring me the best buys. Oh, the people of
Kiniwata all spoke highly of Johnny Lingo. Yet when
they spoke they smiled and the smiles were slightly
mocking.

"Get Johnny Lingo to help you find what you want
and then let him do the bargaining," advised Shenkin as
I sat on the veranda of his guest house and wondered
whether to visit Nurabandi. "He'll earn his commission
four times over. Johnny Lingo knows values and how to
make a deal."

"Johnny Lingo!" The chubby boy on the veranda
steps hooted the name, then hugged his knees and
rocked with shrill laughter.

"St-t," said his father and the laughter grew silent,
revealed only by the quivering of the small back.
"Johnny Lingo's the sharpest trader in this part of the
Pacific."

The simple statement made the boy choke and almost
roll off the steps. Smiles broadened on the faces of the
villagers standing near by.

"What goes on?" I demanded. "Everybody around
here tells me to get in touch with Johnny Lingo and then

breaks up. Is it some kind of trick, a wild-goose chase, like sending someone for a left-handed wrench? Is there no such person or is he the village idiot or what? Let me in on the joke."

"There's no joke," said Shenkin. "When we tell you to see Johnny, it's good advice."

"Then why all the winking and snickering? And what —" I pointed to the still-convulsed child, "— brought out the hyena in him?"

"That one has no respect for his elders. Go inside and be foolish," he ordered. "Tell your mother to find you some useful work."

The boy obediently scrambled to his feet, but passing his father, he paused to whisper impudently, "Did you tell him also, Papa, he should see the wife of Johnny Lingo?" Then, in high glee, he fled into the house as his father's broad palm almost, but not quite, made contact with his brown bottom.

I waited till the hour after the afternoon sleep when a long cool glass and the beginning of shadows encouraged conversation. Then I asked my host again why they mocked at Johnny Lingo.

"They like to laugh." He shrugged his heavy shoulders. "And Johnny's the brightest, the quickest, the strongest young man in all this group of islands. And, for his age, the richest. So they like best to laugh at him."

"But if he's all you say, all everybody says, what is there to laugh about?"

Only one thing. Five months ago, at fall festival time, Johnny came to Kiniwata and found himself a wife. He paid her father eight cows!"

He spoke the last words with great solemnity and I

knew enough about island customs to be thoroughly impressed. Two or three cows would buy a fair-to-middling wife, four or five a highly satisfactory one.

"Good grief!" I said. "Eight cows! She must have beauty that takes your breath away."

She's not ugly," he conceded, and smiled a little, well pleased with my reaction. "But the kindest could only call Sarita plain. She was three months past marriage age when Johnny came and no one had offered for her. Unless you count the widower Ben Panjay, who's older than her father. He put up one cow and might have gone to two, but she shrank so when he touched her that he took back his bid. Old Sam Karoo, her father, was beginning to be afraid she'd be left on his hands."

But then he got eight cows for her? Isn't that an extraordinary number?"

"Never been paid before on Kiniwata or any neighboring island. Did you notice the girl who brought the fruit this morning? Of course you did."

And of course I had. "The tall one?" I asked.

"The tall one," he agreed, and curved his hands through the air in a more graphic description.

"She's magnificent," I said. "Is she Johnny's —"

"Oh, no." He shook his head. "Sarita's on Nurabandi. She's not been back since she married. I only mention the girl of the fruit because she's the most beautiful woman on the island. If you appreciate her now, you should have seen her last year, before she was married. Ah-h!" He let out his breath in a long sign. "She brought her father seven cows, with four men bidding."

"Yes Johnny paid eight and you call his wife plain?"

"I said it would be kindness to call her plain. She was

little and skinny with no — ah — endowments. She walked with her head ducked and her shoulders hunched, as if she was trying to hide behind herself. Her cheeks had no color, her eyes never opened beyond a slit and her hair was a tangled mop half over her face. She was scared of her own shadow, frightened by her own voice. She was afraid to speak up or laugh in public. She never romped with the girls, so how could she attract the boys?"

"But she attracted Johnny?"

"Yes, there's no denying that. He sat beside her on the first night of the festival and walked home with her, the long way. And on the seventh day he met her father to make a marriage contract. The village has been open-mouthed ever since."

"It's queer," I admitted, "but not impossible. Those shy timid girls quite often appeal to strong men. It happens all over the world. There's just no accounting for love."

"That's true enough," said the fat man. "Why this one loves that and another will have only someone else is a puzzle no sane man would try to explain. So we accepted Johnny's falling in love with Sarita. But when he paid her father eight cows — "

"Oh yes." I'd forgotten the cows. "How do you explain that?"

"We don't. And that's why the villagers grin when they talk about Johnny. They got a bang out of remembering that he came to Kiniwata and paid eight cows for a girl anyone here could have had for one or two. And they get a special satisfaction from the fact that Johnny, who's called the sharpest trader in the islands, was bested by dull old Sam Karoo."

"But there must have been something special about the girl. Has she an inheritance or —"

"She'll inherit Sam's eight cows, if he still owns them when he dies. Nothing more."

"Then why?"

"That's what no one knows and everyone wonders. Some, the women mostly, say he was so blind with love he agreed to Sam's first figure. But how would Sam ever think of asking more for Sarita than has been paid before for any woman? Others suspect some kind of trickery, say that maybe there was something in the marriage cup that muddled Johnny's brain. But Sam's not smart enough for trickery. Besides, he seems as baffled by what happened as any of us. And the cousins who went with him to the marriage meeting tell the same story he does."

"What is the story?"

All the way to the Council tent the cousins were urging Sam to try for a good settlement. Ask for three cows, they told him, and hold out for two until you're sure he'll only pay one. But Sam was in such a stew and so afraid that there'd be some slip in this marriage chance for Sarita that they knew he wouldn't hold out for anything. So while they waited they resigned themselves to accepting one cow and thought instead of their luck in getting such a good husband for Sarita. Then Johnny came into the tent, and, without waiting for a word from any of them, went straight up to Sam Karoo, grasped his hand and said, 'Father of Sarita, I offer eight cows for your daughter." Sam thought he was making game of him and tried to pull away. But Johnny held on till the father and the cousins were all convinced that he'd gone mad and they'd better seal the contract before he came to his senses."

"And he delivered the cows?"

"At once. They were waiting outside the tent, all eight of them. The wedding was that same evening and as soon as it was over Johnny took Sarita to the island of Cho for the first week of marriage. Then they went home to Narabundi and we haven't seen them since. Except at festival time, there's not much travel between the islands."

"Eight cows," I said unbelievingly. "And that girl with the fruit was only worth seven. I'd like to meet Johnny Lingo."

"That's what we've all been telling you." My host's grin was wide. "You should meet Johnny. For many reasons."

I wanted fish, I wanted vegetables, I wanted pearls, so the next afternoon I beached my boat at Narabundi. And I noticed with passing interest as I asked directions to the five-room house of Johnny Lingo that the mention of his name brought no sly smile to the lips nor even a twinkle to the eyes of his fellow Narabundians. And when I met the slim, serious young man, when he welcomed me to his home with a grace that made me feel the owner, I was glad that from his own people he had respect unmingled with mockery. Seeing him then, so earnest, so sober, so unlikely to go mad, I wondered even more what had made him behave with such recklessness on Kiniwata.

We sat on softly plaited bamboo chairs in the main room of his house and talked of the things I wanted. He agreed to guide me to good fishing, to sell me vegetables, to bargain for pearls. And then he said: "You come here from Kiniwata?"

And I said, yes, that was where I'd been told to look him up.

"They speak much of me on that island?"

"Yes," I said. "They say there's almost nothing I might want that you can't help me get."

He smiled gently. "My wife is from Kiniwata."

"Yes, I know."

"They speak much of her?"

"A little."

"What do they say?"

"Why, just —" The question caught me off balance. "They told me her name and who her father was and that you were married at fall festival time."

"Nothing more?" The curve of his eyebrows told me he knew there had to be more.

"They also say the marriage settlement was eight cows?" I paused, then went on, coming as close as I could to a direct question. "They wonder why."

"They say that?" His eyes lighted with pleasure. He seemed not to have noticed the question. "Everyone in Kiniwata knows about the eight cows?"

I nodded.

"And in Narabundi everyone knows it, too." His chest expanded with satisfaction. "Always and forever, when they speak of marriage settlements, it will be remembered that Johnny Lingo paid eight cows for Sarita."

So that's the answer, I thought with disappointment. All this mystery and wonder and the explanation's only vanity. It's not enough for his ego to be known as the smartest, the strongest, the quickest. He had to make himself famous for his way of buying a wife. I was tempted to deflate him by reporting that in Kiniwata he was laughed at for a fool.

And then I saw her. Through the glass-beaded portieres that shimmered in the archway, I watched her enter the adjoining room to place a bowl of blossoms on the dining table. She stood still a moment to smile with sweet gravity at the young man beside me. Then she went swiftly out again. And she was the most beautiful woman I have ever seen. Not with the beauty of the girl who carried fruit. That now seemed cheap, common, earthbound. This girl had an eternal loveliness that was at the same time from the heart of nature. The dew-fresh flowers with which she'd pinned back her lustrous black hair accented the glow of her cheeks. The lift of her shoulders, the tilt of her chin, the sparkle of her eyes all spelled a pride to which no one could deny her the right. And as she turned to leave she moved with a lithe grace that made her look like a queen who might, with enchantment, turn into a kitten.

When she was out of sight I turned back to Johnny Lingo and found him looking at me with eyes that reflected the pride in the girl's.

"You admire her?" he murmured.

"She — she's glorious. Who is she?"

"My wife."

I stared at him blankly. Was this some custom I had not heard about? Had he, for the price of eight cows, bought both Sarita and this other? Before I could form a question he spoke again.

"That is Sarita."

"But she's not the Sarita from Kiniwata," I said.

"There is only one Sarita." His way of saying the words gave them a special significance. "Perhaps you wish to say she does not look the way they say she looked in Kiniwata."

"She doesn't. The impact of the girl's appearance made me forget tact. "I heard she was homely, or at least nondescript. They all make fun of you because you let yourself be cheated by Sam Karoo."

"You think he cheated me? You think eight cows were too many?" A slow smile slid over his lips as I shook my head. "Soon it will be the spring festival and I will take my Sarita back to Kiniwata. She can see her father and her friends again. And they can see her. Do you think anyone will make fun of us then?"

"Not likely. But I don't understand. How can she be so different from the way she was described?"

"She has been five months away from Kiniwata. Much has happened to change her. Much in particular happened the day she went away."

"You mean she married you?"

"That, yes. But most of all, I mean the arrangements for the marriage."

"Arrangements?"

"Do you ever think," he asked reflectively, "What it must mean to a women to know that her husband has met with her father to settle the lowest price for which she can be bought? And then later, when all the women talk, as women do. They boast of what their husbands paid for them. One says four cows, another maybe six. How does she feel, the woman who was sold for one or two? This could not happen to my Sarita."

"Then you paid that unprecedented number of cows just to make your wife happy?"

"Happy?" He seemed to turn the word over on his tongue, as if to test its meaning. "I wanted Sarita to be happy, yes, but I wanted more than that. You say she's different from the way they remember her in Kiniwata. This is true. Many things can change a woman. Things that happen inside, things that happen outside. But the thing that matters most is what she thinks about herself. In Kiniwata, Sarita believed she was worth nothing. Now she knows she is worth more than any other woman on the islands."

"Then you wanted —"

"I wanted to marry Sarita. I loved her and no other woman."

"But —" I was close to understanding.

"But," he finished softly," I wanted an eight-cow wife."

Chapter Twenty

About Love

C. Douglas Beardall

T hey sat together on the porch steps, so close that their moon-shadow was a single wedge of blackness against the weathered wood. Tomorrow was the wedding, with all the excitement and confusion, tears and laughter. There would be no privacy then. But this quiet hour was their own.

She said, "It's peaceful, isn't it?" She was watching the great stately clouds march over their heads and drop from sight into the quicksilver sea. He was watching her, and thought that he had never seen her so beautiful.

The wind blew; the waves made little hush, hush sounds, sighing against the sand. "You know," she said, "I always wondered how I'd feel the night before my wedding. Scared, or thrilled, or uncertain, or what."

"You're not scared, are you?"

"Oh no," she said quickly. She hugged his arm and put her face against his shoulder in the impulsive way she had. "Just a little solemn, maybe. Solemn and gay, and young and old, and happy and sad. Do you know what I mean?"

"Yes," he said, "I know."

"It's love that does it, I suppose," she said. "That old thing; we've never talked about it much, have we? About love itself, I mean."

He smiled a little, "We never had to."

"I'd sort of like to— now," she said. "Do you mind? I'd like to try to tell you how I feel before tomorrow happens."

"Will it be any different after tomorrow?"

"No, but I may not be able to talk about it then. It may go down somewhere deep inside, below the talking level."

"All right," he said. "Tell me about love."

She watched a cloud ravel itself against the moon. "Well," she said, "to me it's a shining thing, like a golden fire or a silver mist. It comes so very quietly; you can't command it, but you can't deny it, either. When it does come, you can't quite see it or touch it, but you can feel it — inside of you and around you and around the person you love. It changes you, it changes everything. Colors are brighter, music is sweeter, full little honeysuckles are heavenly food, funny things are funnier. Ordinary speech won't do — you grope for better ways to express how you feel. You read poetry. Maybe you even try to write it."

She leaned back clasping her hands around her knees, the moonlight bright and ecstatic on her face.

"Oh, it's so many things. Waltzing in the dark; waiting for the phone to ring, opening the box of flowers. It's holding hands in a movie; it's humming a sad little tune; it's walking in the rain; it's riding in a convertible with the wind in your hair. It's the quarreling and making up again. It's the first warm drowsy thought in the morning and the last kiss at night."

She broke off suddenly and gave him a desolate look. "But it's all been said before, hasn't it?"

"Even if it has," he told her gently, "that doesn't make it any less true."

"Maybe I'm just being silly," she said doubtfully. "Is that the way love seems to you?"

He did not answer for a while. At last he said, "I might add a little to your definition."

"You mean you wouldn't change it?"

"No, just add to it."

She put her chin in her hands. "Go ahead, I'm listening."

He took out the pen she had given him and looked at it for a moment. "You said it was a lot of little things. You're right. I could mention a few that don't have much glitter. But they have an importance that grows."

She watched his lean fingers begin to move. "Tell me," she said.

"Oh, coming home to somebody when the day is ended — or waiting for somebody to come home to you. Giving, or getting, a word of praise when none is really deserved. Sharing a joke that nobody else understands. Planting a tree together and watching it grow. Sitting up with a sick child. Remembering anniversaries. Do I make it sound terribly dull?

She did not say anything; she shook her head.

"Everything you mentioned is part of it," he went on. "But it's not all triumphant, you know. It's also sharing disappointment, and sorrow. It's going out to slay the dragon, and finding the dragon too much for you, and running away — but going out again the next day. It's the little chips of tolerance that you finally knock off the granite of your ego, not saying, "I told you so," not noticing the dented fender on the family car. It's the gradual acceptance of limitations — your own as well as others. It's discarding some of the ambitions you had for yourself, and planting them in your children." His voice trailed off into the glistening night.

"Are you talking," she asked finally, "about living or loving?"

"You'll find," he said, "there's not much of one without the other."

"When — when did you learn that?"

"Quite a while ago, before your mother died." His hand touched her shining hair.

"Better get to bed now, baby. Tomorrow's your big day."

"She clung to him suddenly. "Oh, Daddy, I'm going to miss you so."

"Nonsense," he said gruffly, "I'll be seeing you all the time. Run along now." But after she had gone he sat there for a long time, alone in the moonlight.

About the Authors

Douglas and Jewel Beardall have both served as full-time missionaries. Sister Beardall served in the Frankfurt, West German Mission and Brother Beardall served in the Chicago, Illinois Mission.

After receiving their formal educations at Brigham Young University, they were married in the Salt Lake Temple by Elder LeGrand Richards.

Douglas and Jewel have also written and published *The Qualities of Love, The Missionary Kit, About the Three Nephites, Passage to Light* and various articles which have been published in national magazines, trade journals and periodicals including *The Ensign* magazine.

The Beardall's work in publishing has taken their residence to Southern California, Southern Nevada and Utah where they now reside with their four children; Jeff, Holly, Jennifer and Scott.